Breaking Barriers

10 Entrepreneurial Women Share Their Stories

Trish Tonaj

Manor House

Library and Archives Canada Cataloguing in Publication

Tonaj, Trish, author
    Breaking barriers : 10 entrepreneurial women share their stories / Trish Tonaj.

ISBN 978-1-988058-14-6 (hardback).

ISBN 978-1-988058-13-9 (paperback)

1. Businesswomen. 2. Success in business. I. Title.

HD6053.T66 2016   650.1082   C2016-904808-X

Printed and bound in Canada / First Edition.
Cover Design-layout-Interior-edit: Michael Davie / Trish Tonaj
168 pages. All rights reserved.
Published September 15, 2016
Manor House Publishing Inc.
452 Cottingham Crescent, Ancaster, ON, L9G 3V6
www.manor-house.biz
 (905) 648-2193

"This project has been made possible [in part] by the Government of Canada. « Ce projet a été rendu possible [en partie] grâce au gouvernement du Canada."

Funded by the Government of Canada
Financé par le gouvernement du Canada

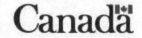

Breaking Barriers / Trish Tonaj

*To the woman who provided inspiration, confidence,
and encouraged a "can do" attitude,
Jacqueline Anne Stevenson,
my biggest cheerleader!*

Gratitude

This book would never have been written without my own "ah ha" moment with 47 other business professionals who gave me the idea to share entrepreneurial stories.

My "light bulb moment" arrived when I was in Boston at Harvard Law School-Negotiation Institute, attending a certificate program on Mediation and Dispute Resolution in the summer of 2015. The Harvard Halls inspired this venture and for that I am truly grateful.

To the Fabulous Women who have shared their stories with no financial remuneration and participated with enthusiasm in support of an idea – my heartfelt thanks. I truly hope the journey has just begun!

To Tricia Hellingman of Hellingman Communications Inc. for her assistance with editing the words to convey the message. Thank you for your time, patience and expertise. To say it takes a village will include your efforts.

I am grateful for friends and family who gave me the courage, love and inspiration to write this book in the wee hours of the morning or late at night with a cup of tea, wearing fluffy slippers after working a full day. It has truly been a labour of love.

Manor House – my thanks for believing in the journey and sharing the message in both digital and print.

To you, for reading the words that may inspire an idea. Good luck, and thank you for sharing your time with all of us.

@phaze2wellness.com

Table of Contents

Cataloguing In Publication 2

Dedication 3

Gratitude 4

Introduction 7

Breaking Barriers – A Few Stats: 10

Business Planning 1, 2, 3 …100 13

Are you an Entrepreneur? 18

Mentorship 24

A Solid Foundation – Your Education 29
Doing What You Love...
Sharon Gilmour Glover – Light-Core

Building an Empire – Having a Dream 45
The Gender Game; Does It Still Exist?
Erin Dunham –The Other Bird

Health and Wellness – Your Personal Plan 57
Invest In You; Your Best Asset
Trish Tonaj – Phaze2inc.

Collaboration – Like-Minded Entrepreneurs 69
Your Journey Begins
Karin Schuett – Circle of Life Cremation and Burial Inc.

Marketing – Become Your Biggest Cheerleader 85
Build Your Personal Brand
Jennifer Kelly – New Initiatives Marketing

Lifestyle Choices – A Balancing Act 97
Your Family in Business
Odile, Kinza, and Gabrielle Nasri – *ça va de soi*

Financial Well-being – Creating a Workbook 107
Organizing Your Financial Statement
Lee Helkie – Helkie Financial & Insurance Services Inc.

The Art of Reinvention: 119
Turning Lemons into Lemonade
The Power of Positive Energy
Gloria MacDonald – Life Alchemy Inc.

Networking – Your Circle of Influence 131
Building Your Personal Tribe
Martha Henderson – Independent Consultant, Arbonne

Expanding Your Territory – The Confidence Game 141
Your Roadmap to Expansion
Virginia Burt – Virginia Burt Designs Inc.

Life Experience 157

Opportunities 162

About the Author 163

Introduction

There are many reasons why people start their own business. The most obvious is of course to make money to sustain a standard of living for the individual and his or her family.

Freedom, excitement and sense of accomplishment are some of the words that are often used when people describe their experience.

There is no discrimination for age, gender or ethnicity; it feeds a basic human element to succeed.

Entrepreneurship is the fastest growing segment of the economy in both Canada and the United States with more and more people joining the ranks of the "self-employed."

In fact, there are over 28-million small businesses in North America with over 50 per cent of the population working in these unique incubators of creativity.

The research is staggering and the statistics speak to a whole host of pros and cons that provide information for the would-be-entrepreneur.

I stumbled upon an interesting independent study completed in 2014, which supported the objectives for writing this book. Amway, a company that has been in business for more than 55 years commissioned its fifth Global Entrepreneurship Report.

More than 43,000 individuals in 38 countries were surveyed to gather stats on the global state of the self-employed.

When reading through the material, the most interesting information was from two target groups:

1) Twenty-eight per cent of those surveyed started a business because of a mentor, and 2) another 24 per cent were inspired by entrepreneurial success stories.

This information had me thinking about my own business experience.

Early in my career, I did have the pleasure of working with a mentor, a gentleman who believed in my entrepreneurial spirit and fed my thirst for independence.

"Mike" was the senior vice-president of merchandising for a national Canadian department store. He took me under his wing and provided an opportunity to learn the fundamentals of business in the *real* world.

I give him a tremendous amount of credit for my success because he recognized my entrepreneurial characteristics at the age of 21. He provided a platform for learning that carried me throughout my career, and I was able to build on that hard-earned education until I was ready to go out on my own.

He didn't make it easy, but rather nurtured and tempered my enthusiasm by guiding me to learn a few practical tools necessary for my personal journey. I gathered information and experience for about 10 years before I took the leap of faith and started my first company.

Mentorship is one of the ways we're able to share life experience – good or bad – to the benefit of another.

Using this as a foundation, I have networked, read, interviewed and learned from a number of successful individuals who each have a very unique story that enriched my journey.

It is with these two things in mind I have approached 10 successful women to share their stories, so that you too can experience the adrenaline rush that sparks an idea for a new adventure or business venture.

These women are from all walks of life and share no connection other than their courage to believe in themselves, start a business and succeed.

They are ordinary women who have extraordinary accomplishments from various fields of expertise. Each will share their thoughts on a particular aspect of entrepreneurship, which tell a story, with the hope of assisting you to find your own inspiration.

"Breaking Barriers" is part of the learning curve and we all agree that you continually need to reinvent yourself to overcome the obstacles that cross your path in a successful business.

Some barriers are systemic and found within an industry, while others are part of the social norms that present themselves each day within the world of business. In other instances, it is a personal barrier that we need to overcome in order to assist with our own definition of success.

We hope you find this *information share* will provide you with a few helpful, tips and tools when you begin your journey.

Enjoy the read; all of the ladies profiled in the following chapters wish you every success in building your dreams.

Breaking Barriers? – A Few Stats:

We live in a time where information is at our fingertips. All you need is to open your computer, and use your phone or tablet to access information. When you are getting ready to start a business, you will most likely complete a business plan, which will include information on your target market.

Before you begin to crunch the numbers you may wish to take a look at the following statistics, which have been compiled from a number of online resources, and represent stats for both Canada and the United States.

The statistics:

- There are almost 28-million small businesses in North America

- More than 50 per cent of the population works in small business

- Small business generates more than 65 per cent of net new jobs

- Seven out of 10 firms survive at least two years

- 52 per cent of firms are home-based businesses

- Women are better than men as money managers

- Women deliver better company performance

- Women achieve a higher than average Return On Investment (ROI)

- Women invest in each other, with 22 per cent offering "Angel Investing"

- Women are building a vibrant, layered ecosystem (e.g. through networking and professional groups)

- Sixty per cent of high-net-worth women have earned their fortunes

- Forty-five per cent of American millionaires are women

- Women NEVER stop learning

- Women use failure as a launching pad to success

- Women lead over a third of the countries' small and medium-sized businesses

- More than 62 per cent own a business in the following three sectors: health care and social assistance; information and cultural industries; and, the arts (includes entertainment, recreation, retail trade, accommodation and food services)

- These owners have more than 10 years of managerial experience

- 18 per cent reported having at least a Master's degree compared to their male counterparts

Although any statistical information may be skewed to a hypothesis, I find it encouraging that entrepreneurship is breaking barriers with women who are taking an active role in their own success.

The women interviewed each have a unique story they are sharing to encourage you to take a chance on your business idea.

Break your own barriers: What is the worst that can happen? If you fail, think of the experience you will have gained and then offer to another company looking for your unique brand, skills and talents.

It's a great resume builder and, if nothing else, you will have a new appreciation for earned success.

These statistics will evolve and new ideas will always be created through the ability to go outside our comfort zones.

Just think of your legacy, and how you and your success will encourage future generations.

Here are a few of the sites visited for information:

www.statcan.gc.ca
www.canadianentrepreneurtraining.com
www.bdc.ca
www.entreprisescanada.ca
www.bis.gov.bdm/entrepreneurship.htm
www.inc.com

Business Planning – 1, 2, 3 ...100

Every successful new business starts with a solid business plan, a road map that becomes a "working document" for the first three years.

Before you put pen to paper, below is a laundry list of questions, by category that you may wish to consider. The stories in the following chapters may assist with the development and structure for your own strategic plan.

You already have a "Great Idea"

Corporate Outline = Business Foundation:

1) What is the name of your business?
2) Have you completed a name search?
3) Will you be a sole proprietor, a partnership or be incorporated?
4) Who will hold the roles of responsibility? (e.g. president, vice-president, secretary)
5) Who is the ultimate decision maker?
6) Do you need a Board of Directors?
7) Who is your target market?
8) What sets you apart from your competition?
9) Have you registered your business name?
10) Where will your business be located?
11) Do you have a mentor or business coach?
12) What professional services do you require? (e.g. lawyer, accountant, bookkeeper, insurance broker, courier company)
13) What types of insurance do you need? (e.g. building contents, liability, disability, errors and omissions)
14) Do you need a professional license?
15) Any government rules-regulations re your industry?

16) What are your revenue sources?
17) Do you need an operations manual?
18) Do you need to copyright or trademark your product or service?
19) Will you develop an advisory board?
20) Have you visited your competition and completed a competitive analysis?
21) When is your "open for business" date?

Financing = Operating Capital:

22) Who will finance your venture?
23) Are you eligible for a grant, start-up capital from the government or angel investor group?
24) Have you opened a bank account and require cheques or a credit card?
25) Who will have signing authority on your accounts?
26) How much working capital is needed in the first year?
27) How will you purchase inventory, manufacture your product or create intellectual property?
28) Do you need to purchase or lease office equipment or computer software?
29) Do you require or have you registered to collect government taxes?
30) Have you arranged for any emergency funds?
31) Are you prepared to expand in the first three years?
32) How will you back up your data?
33) Where will you store your data?
34) What type of data security system do you require?
35) Will you need invoices or sales receipts?
36) Will you accept personal cheques, credit cards, bank transfers, e-commerce?
37) Do you have software/hardware to support your payment terms?
38) Do any memberships or business associations provide discounts or group rates?

39) Will you need to develop a disaster plan or a plan for business interruption services?

Physical Space = Social Structure:

40) If you rent space, what is your strategy to gain visual exposure?
41) Is your location providing customer convenience?
42) Do you have or require a real estate agent, contractor, decorator or architect?
43) What square footage do you need to be efficient?
44) Will there be enough space to expand?
45) Are there any government, city, town or municipal restrictions?
46) Will you need a building permit?
47) What will be your lease term and conditions?
48) Will you have any outdoor signage and are any permits required?
49) Do you need a security system?
50) Do you have adequate parking?

Sales = Your Team:

51) Who will sell your product or service?
52) Do you need employees within the first six months or will you contract services?
53) Are confidentiality, non-compete agreements required?
54) Where will you advertise for a sales team?
55) What is your pricing structure?
56) Will you have employee loyalty or incentive programs?
57) Do you need a training program?
58) What is your compensation package?
59) Will you include employee benefits? (health and medical, pension plan, stock options)
60) How will you establish Key Performance Indicators? (KPIs)

61) How many times per week will your team meet or connect to brainstorm?
62) Have you considered an intern program?
63) How will you target customers?
64) Is your business scaleable to meet consumer demand?
65) Do you need to engage someone with experience in business development as part of the team?
66) Who will handle human resources?

Marketing = Connect with Customers:

67) Do you have a brand strategy?
68) What is your WOW factor?
69) Who is your primary and secondary market?
70) Have you developed a logo?
71) Who will design your business cards and other stationary items?
72) Do you have an online strategy?
73) What is the budget for marketing?
74) Do you require print advertising?
75) What will you offer as a marketing kit or information package for your customers?
76) Will you have a customer recognition or loyalty program?
77) What social media channels will you use?
78) Is social media relevant to your business?
79) How will you communicate with your customers?
80) Do you need a Customer Relationship Management or CRM system?
81) How will you engage your community?
82) Will you be affiliated with a charity?
83) What business or community groups would you like to join?
84) Are there any industry associations where you may become a member?

85) Will you sponsor a team or host a special event?
86) Who will be your creative director or provide innovative ideas?
87) Who will coordinate your IT requirements?
88) Do you require additional education, upgrades or continuing education credits?
89) Will you have a soft opening or a grand opening celebration?

Peace of Mind = Personal/Family Care:

90) How will you achieve work/life balance?
91) How will you determine your success?
92) Do you need a personal coach or assistant?
93) Do you have a mentor?
94) How many days per week and hours per day are you able to work?
95) Who will be your biggest cheerleader?
96) When will you be able to plan a vacation?
97) Do you have someone you can rely on in an emergency?
98) Do you have a retirement and/or investment plan?
99) Do you have a Power of Attorney as well as Last Will and Testament?
100) If things don't work out, what is your exit strategy?

Last but not least:

When you've become a success,
what is your succession plan?

Whew!

This *is* a lot to consider, but a good list to use when building your plan for success.

Are You An Entrepreneur?

There has never been a better time to be in business.

Your target market is defined only by your ability to provide a product or service to your audience.

The power of the Internet presents opportunities that did not exist 10 years ago, and we live in a society where easy access to information, products and services is available to all consumers.

Just think how many things in life have changed? Everyday tasks have become easier, faster and more accessible.

We can now read books on a mobile device, share recipes through a tablet, and look for directions, phone numbers and addresses with the click of a button.

Our cars have computers and navigation systems and we have voice-activated phones. Do you remember what a telephone book looks like? How much time did you spend at the library researching your last school project? And when was the last letter you sent to communicate with your friends or family?

Opportunities are limited only by our ability to adapt, change and create ways of communicating with each other.

E-commerce web sites create **trillions** of dollars in revenue, with business transactions completed in the privacy of our offices and homes.

What personal characteristics do we need to succeed? Have the characteristics for success changed as drastically as the business platform?

As entrepreneurs, I believe, if we look in the mirror we will see the basics are the same. Core characteristics we identify as foundational elements are present in each individual entrepreneur in order to succeed.

These core values and traits are part of our personal foundation. Identifying those qualities will give us an opportunity to ensure we are the best we can be, as we plan for the future and embark on one of the most exciting journeys in our career.

After much discussion and collaboration, I've listed below characteristics I believe are present in every entrepreneur:

1) Competitive
2) Confident
3) Curious
4) Decisive
5) Flexible
6) Good Listener
7) Organized
8) Passionate
9) Persistent
10) Trusting

1) Competitive

Having a competitive edge is necessary to succeed in selling your product or service. Every customer in our target market is looking for something different that provides value = value proposition. In a global economy we need to ensure our offering is crystal clear and easily understood.

As entrepreneurs, we must think competitively so we're always "on our game." Being competitive will encourage innovation to stay current and relevant in today's business climate. Competition and innovation are the one-two combination that will drive our personal success engine.

2) Confident

Believing in yourself can give you a healthy dose of confidence. Having the vision to see yourself achieving your goals and objectives will ensure success. Having confidence in both our successes and failures will be necessary for long-term growth and viability. There will be things that will not go as planned - having the confidence to learn from our failures as well as our success will keep us on track and moving forward towards our ultimate goals.

3) Curious

Give me an entrepreneur who isn't curious and, well, you don't have an entrepreneur. The ability to think "outside the box" results from being curious. Finding a better way to do something drives the success engine.

Just think of the number of things that have changed over the last five years and you can actually visualize the wheels of curiosity at work. Building a better mousetrap has fundamentally fuelled change for centuries, and it explains why we constantly find ourselves in a new place in time. Being curious will keep us current.

4) Decisive

The ability to make a decision in a timely manner is critical to our being leaders, not followers. Taking raw data and not only understanding this information, but also making the best decision for your company, is a skill honed through time. Some use their "gut instinct" as a guide when considering various components for a sound decision.

A decisive leader creates an atmosphere of confidence and, as your company grows, your team will support and follow your direction based on your ability to be decisive with sound judgment.

5) Flexible

Flexible and adaptable go hand in hand. Giving yourself the "wiggle room" to change direction or make a course correction to your strategic plan may be a defining moment in your long-term success.

There may be times when the best plan requires a tweak here and there in order to guarantee a strategic outcome. Being flexible gives you "permission" to change and adapt, with freedom and conviction.

6) Good Listener

Listening and absorbing what you've heard is one of the most challenging of skills or characteristics. The pace of business is fast, and being able to hear information and decipher what is relevant is a gift. Whether you're in a sales meeting with a customer or discussing a new strategy with a member of your team, listening and understanding the words we hear is a fundamental part of making decisions.

There may be times when we need to take a deep breath, review our notes and contemplate our thoughts in order to formulate a plan, but it all begins with listening and understanding what we've heard.

7) Organized

The ability to multi-task is part of life. Organizing the day, week or month, so that we work smarter, not harder, can be challenging.

We rely on tools to assist in our quest for organization. Very few of us go without our PDA, always ready to respond to our customer or team in a timely manner. We feel confident in our ability to respond when we're organized.

8) Passionate

We've all heard the saying "if you love what you do, you'll never work a day in your life." So true. Every entrepreneur has a passion and conviction for their product or service.

They believe in their brand and their emotional connection for their business comes from a strong belief in our value proposition. You may not always love certain day-to-day tasks, but your passion never wanes.

9) Persistent

This quality is one that will provide you with positive building blocks. It will help you conquer fear, provide focus and give you the courage to go forward to the finish line. There will definitely be obstacles to our success and persistence gives us that "little extra something" to go the distance. It creates ingenuity to problem solve, patience to wait for the best opportunities and the conviction to believe that what you are doing is best for you and your family.

10) Trusting

Trust at times may feel like taking a leap of faith. There are so many people you'll need to trust in order for your dream to become a reality. Accountants, bookkeepers, lawyers and perhaps contractors will be a part of your start up. As you grow, sales people, web developers, marketing gurus, event coordinators and perhaps personal assistants will become part of your expansion plans.

The collaboration of individuals you trust will be invaluable to your overall success. Never doubt the people that you come across on your success journey; they will add value to your experience. Trusting in your circle of influence will not only assist with your success but perhaps even become an integral part of the formula.

These 10 qualities or characteristics are by no means a definitive list and you may find that you have a whole host of other attributes that will be of benefit as you embark on your own journey.

What this list will do is give you a few things to consider as you formulate your plan and get ready to step outside your comfort zone into the land of entrepreneurship or business expansion.

One of the key elements that ties all of these qualities together is the ability to see where we need to personally develop and expand our resources.

For some, you may simply need a family member or friend to brainstorm, bounce ideas off of, and receive feedback. For others, it may be a mentor or coach.

There is no better exercise than finding a success partner – someone who will hold us accountable and provide encouragement when we need it most. I have heard many refer to this person as a "wingman."

It's the one person with whom we feel most comfortable and will be there – not only when we are successful but also when we fail. Often, that same person will be our biggest cheerleader.

If you can find that unique someone when you begin your journey, I'm sure you will find that this person will allow you to look in the mirror and see that you have become a better entrepreneur.

Your success depends on a number of characteristics that will change through time having an impact on both you and your business.

Mentorship

To begin the journey we must understand the reason for sharing information and what we hope to accomplish. If you Google the word "mentorship" you'll find this definition:

Mentorship is a relationship in which a more experienced or more knowledgeable person guides a less experienced or less knowledgeable person. The **mentor** may be older or younger, but has a certain area of expertise.

As a noun:

1) a wise and trusted counsellor or teacher

2) an influential senior sponsor or supporter

Its origin:

We acquired "mentor" from the literature of ancient Greece. In Homer's epic *The Odyssey*, Odysseus was away from home fighting and journeying for 20 years. During that time, Telemachus, the son he left as a baby grew up under the supervision of Mentor, an old and trusted friend. When the goddess Athena decided it was time to complete the education of young Telemachus, she visited him disguised as Mentor and they set out together to learn about his father. Today, we use the word *mentor* for anyone who is a positive, guiding influence in another person's life.

One of our greatest pleasures is meeting new people, sharing stories and experiences that give us the opportunity to shape who we are as individuals.

The experiences we share create the fabric of our legacy and give us the content for our own autobiography. When we begin our careers we have a plan or goal that fuels the energy we need to pursue our dreams, and eventually we understand that everyone has a unique story.

As an entrepreneur, the "risk and reward" we experience is tempered with an adrenaline rush that is married to our success and sense of accomplishment.

As a mentor, sharing information to benefit another takes courage, patience and enthusiasm for our own journey. This is a person who is willing to share not only the successes, but failures that shape and form a career.

We are sharing the stories of 10 Entrepreneurial Women who believe in the spirit of mentorship. We are ordinary women who have taken the risk and reward to start a business with a dream. We now enjoy success, however we all took a leap of faith and have had our share of "bumps in the road." Most of us will work for many years to come and expect that the bumps in the road will continue. To be quite honest, that's what makes owning our own business interesting! For most, at one stage in our career, we have enjoyed the experience of a mentor. This is someone who was able to identify something special in all of us and was able to provide a positive influence by offering their expertise and guidance.

While completing research on the topic, I came across the *Ten Commandments of a Mentor* from a company in the United States called Management Mentors, located just outside of Boston, Massachusetts. (How ironic, the very city that provided my "ah ha" moment to write this book!)

1. Facilitate, not clone
2. Uniqueness is important
3. Consistency is critical
4. Faking it is not making it. Provide honest feedback
5. Empower rather than solve
6. You're not responsible alone, you share responsibility

7. Appreciate what you're giving
8. It's not coaching; it's mentoring
9. Honour your limits and boundaries
10. Listening is hard, but advice is easy
    (We could all use more listeners in the world)

Great advice for those who share their story to benefit others!

http://www.management-mentors.com/resources/mentoring-process-mentor?

It is interesting to note, that the idea of mentorship is also used in companies to grow and develop young talent who are interested in furthering their career within an organization they feel is in alignment with their own philosophy. After all, we trade goods and services for compensation that provides us with a lifestyle we enjoy. When we hire an employee, or work with other businesses, we are in fact creating a relationship with other professionals based on sharing information.

A form of mentorship?

In today's business climate we find that the spirit of mentorship is no longer top of mind. Many times we work from a satellite or home office, limiting our ability to work with people who can share their expertise and give us the opportunity to learn from each other.

The downsizing of work teams has been prevalent since 2008 with economies of scale dictating smaller and more efficient organizations. There are a number of statistics that support employee retention based on someone's ability to learn new skills in a challenging work environment. Regardless of age, there is empowerment from learning something new that gives us confidence and provides a sense of accomplishment.

A level of interest is created when an individual reaches out to learn not from a book, computer or textbook but from the experience of another. It takes a curious, open mind who is interested in fostering a relationship based on sharing information through experience from someone they respect.

How do you find a mentor?

There may be times when we learn from someone we never meet but find that person's work inspirational. We may read a book or watch a movie that created an interest in learning more about their life and work. There may be other times when we appreciate the experience of another and then seek to find a mentor who can increase our knowledge and expand our business experience.

I have a fondness for Coco Chanel. She has been an inspiration to me since I was in high school. I have read many books to learn more about her story and even had the pleasure of visiting her suite at The Ritz Charlton in Paris, where she lived for over thirty years until she died on January 10, 1971. Visiting her atelier in Paris was something that will forever be part of my memories. Not only was the hotel spectacular but her sense of style was evident in the way she lived while at The Ritz. She was a woman, who changed the landscape for women with her innovation, determination and drive to succeed. She survived the war and was able to reinvent her business many times from knitwear to couture – including fragrance, jewellery and accessories to become iconic in the world of fashion. She has been my mentor, because of her sense of style, creativity and innovation. The obstacles she overcame in her journey are both inspiring and motivating.

There are many talented individuals who are interested in sharing their stories. All it takes is the connection through an introduction, e-mail or phone call. Most people are happy to share their experience for the benefit of another and all it takes is the courage to ask for help.

Wouldn't it be nice if we were able to learn from each other?

The ladies participating in this book, are sharing their stories, with the hope of inspiring you to embark on your own journey of success.

There is a quote by Coco Chanel that speaks not only of entrepreneurship but the spirit of the journey.

Although directed at "a girl," it speaks to every individual who has a sense of adventure:

"A girl should be two things: classy and fabulous.
In order to be irreplaceable one must always be different.
The most courageous act is still to think for yourself.
Aloud.
Dress shabbily and they will remember the dress;
dress impeccably and they remember the woman.
Fashion is not something that exists in dresses only.
Fashion is in the sky, in the street, fashion has to do with ideas, the way we live, what is happening.
Simplicity is the keynote to all true elegance.
A women who doesn't wear perfume has no future.
Some people think luxury is the opposite of poverty.
It is not.
It is the opposite of vulgarity.
Fashion is architecture: it is a matter of proportions."

This was spoken by a women who developed a brand that's been in existence for more than 50 years, who had a vision with the drive, determination and discipline to succeed.

An inspirational mentor!

A Solid Foundation – Your Education
Doing What You Love...
Sharon Gilmour-Glover – Light-Core

Sharon is chief implementation officer at Light-Core and if you had to describe her in five words or less you would say: "She is a glass half-full kind of person." She is always able to find the positive in every situation, and has the ability to trouble shoot the best solution or resolution to any challenge she has faced in life. This philosophy finds its roots in her belief of the importance of education and the concept of life-long learning. She is a resilient strategic thinker who is generous and humble in her quest to help others.

To hear Sharon describe her personal philosophy: "Education, at its best, helps us to uncover who we are, how we learn, what motivates us and where we can be the best "us" in the world."

The work she does on a day-to-day basis, is actually somewhat different from her formal education. Her undergraduate degree is in outdoor recreation with a focus on interpretation and natural science. She also has a degree in Bachelor of Education and, as part of her Masters of Adult Education studies, conducted graduate level research in adult education - with a focus on entrepreneurship, adult and transformational learning. Within this discipline she also focused on the complexity theory. Sharon will admit she withdrew from the Masters program without getting her third degree, because she simply ran out of time. She was eager to get started in the field of education and felt she had learned all she could from the course.

At that stage, she felt the time spent writing and defending a thesis would be better served applying what she had learned in a practical setting.

Her first career, as an environmental educator, was directly related to her formal education. She chose to work in environmental/outdoor and earth education because she has a deep connection with our planet and wanted to contribute to making the world a better place. The more she learned through school and work experiences, the deeper she came to know herself. She realized that what she did when teaching, was to reflect the potential she saw in her students and mirror it back to them. Her mission was to help them find their own path and plant the seeds of how they could achieve their true potential.

Through her experience she came to realize that an individual's self-awareness would increase based on their surroundings. As each learner came to understand how everything in life is connected, he or she would begin to change and sometimes, transform. The idea of interconnectedness – of life on earth, of people in systems, of everything, man-made or natural was the beginning of her own future career.

Sharon feels education serves us best when we are fully engaged with the concepts we've learned. When we give ourselves to the process of learning, we either end up directly using our education in a practical application, or applying what we've learned to a totally different discipline.

She believes any education will never be a waste of time but rather can become our greatest asset.

The things we seek to learn through education, shape and form who and what we are as individuals.

What resulted from this understanding is that people shape and form a company, not the product or service. Business, is a system and a lever to create meaningful, sustained, transformational change - but its the team of people responsible for the outcome and success of the business. The people you work with day to day affect both the attitude and productivity within the company. It was at this time that Sharon knew she had to find a way to apply what she'd learned to help people achieve their full potential, and use the work they do as a vehicle for change in a global market.

Sharon will admit she never intentionally set out to start her own business. In fact, she had been working in her company for six years before she had an "ah ha" moment and identified with herself as an entrepreneur. Until that time, she felt she was an educator who happened to own and work in business.

Light-Core provides companies with solutions to complex problems and works with people who have a bigger purpose than making money.

The company's clients have a deep-rooted desire to make a significant, positive impact through their work - whether they are owners, non-owning executives or employees with influence. Sharon calls them "game changers," working with individuals looking for sustainable profitable revenue and taking a holistic approach to their business. She connects various elements of their company to their mindset, clearly identifying not only what they do but how they do it, and aligns these core principles with an outcome – providing a product or service.

Her customers experience tremendous growth through this complex process of vertical learning.

She uses her background in education to develop systems for sustainable growth and then coaches teams to work through the barriers they often face when transitioning through a new strategic plan.

Here is a chart that outlines the theory:

Legacy Approach	Light-Core's Approach
Attempt to control outcomes by controlling chaos	Teach clients how to manage themselves in chaos, then teach others
One-size fits all consultant controlled	"Best-practices" replaced by context-based learning frameworks
Often inflexible & prescriptive	Tailored to fit client's view of how his or her world works
Memorizing a particular expert's rules & steps	Learn to identify & resolve unconscious biases & barriers in your business and in yourself
Direction & strategy come from the top	Leaders at all levels learn how to establish new direction, align key stakeholders to the new direction and then how to take the courageous action needed to sustain improved performance – sustained, profitable revenue

Sharon connects the dots between education and business with this insightful explanation: "The education we receive in formal settings and informally through experience, help us uncover our passion and purpose. At its best, it feeds self-awareness. When our work is tied directly to our core purpose, it is a completely different experience than when we are just doing a job."

For some, this would explain the quote we've all heard: "If you love what you do then you'll never work a day in your life." The passion and conviction that comes from working in a career that is exciting and fulfilling is much better than doing a job day after day, no matter how satisfying the pay check. People excel when doing what they love. On every level they have a better understanding and confidence in their contribution not only to their work - but to society. They just feel better about what they do!

That is not to say that you will enjoy everything about your work, nor does it mean that you will excel in all aspects of your business. You may have a natural affinity or strength for sales, marketing, administration operations, research and development, or human resources. To compensate for your weaknesses, or the things you don't enjoy doing, you will then need to connect with individuals that are passionate in other areas of business. These individuals must also be just as committed to success as you are and align with your core philosophy in order for the company as a whole to achieve sustainable growth and profitability. Connecting like-minded individuals as a team working for the same company and towards the same goal, confirms the formula for success.

When I first heard Sharon's theory it just simply made sense. When we connect with people who excel in their area of expertise and work together on the same game plan just think what we can accomplish?

The first step in this transformation is recognizing that you need to change, to understand your core strengths and who you can align with to create a well-rounded team.

To take your company to the next level of excellence you need to ensure that all of the moving parts are working at their best, and towards the same solution. Sharon would like to share some of this learning and you can choose two of the following three modules complementary from her web site: Core Values; How Innovation Ready are You?; and, Changed Thinking, Changed Results.

This is where Sharon and her team are able to provide the tools to take your company to a whole new level of success.

Sharon practices what she preaches and is currently expanding her sphere of influence by taking on various licensees within a global market. She will admit that business development has been her biggest challenge. For her company to achieve multi-millions of dollars in revenue, she has to take her current model and duplicate the concepts with others just as passionate about her corporate philosophy. They must be people of influence who are able to transform organizations through a similar model for change.

She currently has one licensee in Manila, Philippines, who takes a people-centric approach to business. She is in early talks with a potential strategic alliance in Singapore and is traveling to Asia in 2016 to support these new opportunities.

Sharon has spent a great deal of time structuring the various strategic elements she offers to be transferable to other, like-minded entrepreneurs. This will allow her to build her own strategic partnerships, and utilize the skills and experience of people in other cultures, to assist local companies who are expanding in a global market.

Sharon feels the economic crisis in 2008 provided the platform for her unique approach to transformational change. Individuals in business are now taking a hands-on approach to working for companies that are making a difference, not only in the lives of their employees, but in the products and services they provide. We see the trend through the eco conscious mindset of individuals who would like the world to be a better place, safer for the planet and mindful of our natural resources.

To ensure our companies are sustainable, we must first take a look at the individuals that complete a management team. At the core of every successful business are a group of individuals who believe in their own expertise and trust that their colleagues are also committed to the success of the company. With a background in education, Sharon understands that who we are and what we represent changes through time; as people we need to constantly work on our own mindset. Understanding where we want to go in life depends on our ability to navigate the changes that occur and evolve through time, making the necessary changes when required through self- reflection.

Here are a few of the practical tools that Sharon offers to anyone who is interested in sustainable change:

√ gratitude journal

√ personal coach

√ finding your portfolio of passions

√ peer groups

Gratitude Journal

Sharon is self-reflective and does a number of activities to keep herself focused using a monitoring system to track her progress. She completes a weekly check-in with three goals set the previous week, journaling her progress and aligning with those goals. When she has successfully achieved each goal she can then build on her success, altering her path and working towards a life long goal of change and transformation. It is best described as a fluid process.

Personal Coach

Sharon finds that sales and business development have been her biggest obstacle so she is working with a sales coach who assists with a workable plan and weekly reporting to ensure she stays on track. She finds this to be a great way to motivate herself and increase awareness in an area of her business that needs constant change. After all, sales are dynamic and constantly evolving. It is certainly one area of business that is in constant motion.

Portfolio of Passions

This is a new theory for Sharon, and started when she became exhausted, showing signs of burn out - working too many hours and never taking time for herself. In order to change her mindset she wrote down all of the things that she enjoys and began working them into her schedule. This allows her to focus on leisure time throughout the week. Such as taking control of her work schedule, weekends off, riding horses three times per week, getting to bed at a certain hour, reading books, and watching movies. These were, everyday things that will assist with recharging her batteries.

Peer Groups

Sharon belongs to two peer groups. Their members meet monthly to support, encourage and challenge each other to keep moving forward and find ways to navigate through life's inevitable barriers. She is adamant that a peer group must include individuals who are able to provide constructive criticism and at the same time relate to challenges. They also need to be able to take participants out of their comfort zone and provide insight into how to transition through the cycle of change. Positive feedback should be respectful and encouraged for growth and development. This supports her theory that we learn and develop throughout our lives, and not just through formal education.

Here is a story from Sharon on how her own career has changed and evolved throughout the years, and has been influenced by learning or adapting new theories: "I had a blinding flash of personal insight walking along Lakeshore Road in Oakville, Canada in the spring of 1993. I had just met my future husband Tim a few months previously. He was a career business person. I had left my teaching career the previous December to find a way to earn my living in music. For most of my career I had taught Earth Education from a deep ecology perspective, along with leadership and a short stint as a Grade 5 teacher. I knew nothing about business, except that I was usually on the other side of an environmental issue from "Business."

Tim gave me a special edition of a journal called, *New Traditions in Business.* The theme for this special edition was Spirit and Leadership in the 21st Century. I hadn't heard of any of the authors but I had heard of the universities and companies they represented.

The entire edition was dedicated to exploring the many ways business was going to have to change moving into the 21st century. The authors all agreed that the industrial model of profit at any cost, people as cogs in a machine and an expense to be reduced etc., needed to change.

They felt that in order to sustain success, businesses were going to have to embrace people as their greatest asset. That true, principled leadership was going to have to replace leadership focused on creating short-term increases in profit. That business would have to benefit all of humanity and the planet. They had no idea how all of that was going to be accomplished at the same time as generating sustained profit. They just knew it had to be done.

"I was stunned. I had no idea this kind of conversation was happening anywhere in the business community. I had some significant emotional responses to the essays in this journal, which culminated with me stopping dead in the middle of the sidewalk on the north side of Lakeshore Road on a warm, sunny spring day. I knew my life's purpose was to work in business because I had part of the answer.

I knew I had to find a way to get to the tables where these conversations were happening and contribute with my voice.

I didn't start what is now Light-Core until 2001. I did some training and a bit of consulting in the early 90s but it wasn't time. I went off and concentrated on music and found my way back to business in 1999 or 2000. I started the business that has grown into Light-Core when I started getting some clarity on how, specifically, I could help businesses grow. Four months after I started, Tim got an opportunity to join me with a small book of business. We started working together, combining his finance/behaviour-based strategy expertise with my transformational learning/implementation expertise. Fifteen years later, here we are."

Sharon's current goal is to expand her business with a sales target of 20 million. Experiencing changes within her own team, she found herself responsible for sales and business development. She has been able to forecast revenue with clear objectives but she did not have a solid sales plan to match her objectives for growth. She was overwhelmed with blind terror at the thought of selling. She became tongue-tied every time anyone asked about her business. She had NO idea what to say, how to capture her value proposition, or how to communicate what is actually a complex and sophisticated blend of modalities and methodologies in a way that was relevant to a prospective client.

She didn't have the first clue where to find prospects and most devastating of all, she didn't believe she could sell her success despite the fact that the average return on investment or ROI experienced by her clients is between 40 and 150 per cent.

It took her almost a year to strategize and define a short, value proposition that would clearly communicate her business to a potential client in a clear concise manner. For Sharon, this would become her "elevator speech" - a short three-second statement that opens the door for future conversation:

"We help businesses double and triple in size and profitably by helping people learn to manage in chaos."

This would provide her with a starting point to qualify a sale and then allow her to expand into the nuts and bolts of the various theories. Sharon's title as chief implementation officer immediately reinforces the philosophy of her company. In addition to her elevator speech, her business card sends a distinct message that you are dealing with a very different organization. It creates an interest that captures attention in learning more about both Sharon and her company.

Recently at a conference, when asked what businesses need to succeed at exporting, Mairead Lavery, senior vice-president, Business Development Group at Export Development Canada said that in order to succeed, leaders need knowledge, a network of right-fit people and management capacity.

Sharon clearly identified with this suggestion and was able to pinpoint with her own challenge regarding business development which was a combination of a lack of right-fit people in her own network and a very small management capacity. She had already begun her plan for sustainable change and this statement validated her claim and goal.

After applying the methodology that she uses with clients to her own business, at the end of that critical year she was proud to say she was at 100 per cent of her current sales target, with a solid plan for growth and development. She had developed a strategic sales value proposition, which provided a solid framework for the next three years. It is a plan that will take her to achieving her own sustainable profitable revenue. This was no small feat, considering just a short year before she was paralyzed with fear at the overwhelming responsibility for sales.

One of the things that Sharon attributes to her success is concentrating on these three key words: Self-awareness, Purpose and Resilience.

Henry Ford said, "Whether you think you can, or you can't, you're right."

"The success we've achieved in our business and the success we've helped clients achieve, is all premised on a fundamental belief that if it's presenting itself, then it is possible, whatever it is."

She provides a few questions for us to consider when realigning our goals and objectives: What do you believe? Are you willing to engage with the results you get as feedback? That means all of the results, the good, the bad and the ugly. Are you willing to transform - to leave the safety of the world you can see and feel you can control?

If you are, then you will succeed. If you aren't, at some point you will stop moving towards your vision of success because you will lack the conviction to get you there. Sometime stepping out of our comfort zone provides the roadmap to the exact target in our plan.

Sharon often looks back on her own strategic plan and ensures that her path to life long learning includes seminars and workshops that contribute to her continued commitment to education and experiential learning.

Attending these sessions also connects you with your business community and provides an opportunity to share ideas and brainstorm with colleagues, ultimately finding the solution that works best for you and your strategic goals. A great growth experience!

As part of Sharon's contribution to the business community her banker submitted her name for the RBC Canadian Women Entrepreneur Awards. The collective impact of our country's female entrepreneurs cannot be overstated.

The RBC Canadian Women Entrepreneur Awards is the premier national awards program that celebrate the achievements of the most successful in this inspiring group.

Now in its 23rd year, more than 120 women have been recognized for demonstrating excellence from economic growth to social change, from local to global reach and across multiple sectors.

This award celebrates the achievements of a woman who, in a minimum of three years and a maximum of five years, has developed her business into one that's ready for the next level of growth. Since starting the business, the recipient has been successful in building a profitable business and a comprehensive and sustainable business plan.

Sounds like the same foundation that Light-Core uses in its own business model.

Sharon became a semi-finalist amongst the group of other Canadian Female business owners in the category of Micro-Business. By definition a micro-business will focus on an enterprise with less than 10 employees including the entrepreneur. It would have been started with less than $50,000 in capital although can scale into a larger organization based on their product or service. The annual revenue is usually less than $3-million, family owned and operated.

Even through Sharon's company is considered small and entrepreneurial, the results her clients achieve through their own growth and development is certainly top of the line.

Her banker was also female and mentioned that one of the reasons that she nominated Sharon was because she was always up front and forthright about her company's financial circumstances and proactive with their future pans for growth and development.

She was always willing to share new business ideas, strategies and had developed a strong personal relationship with the bank. This line of communication created a level of confidence and support with the key decision makers at the bank throughout the various stages of their own growth and development.

Proud Semi-Finalist of the 2015 RBC Canadian Women Entrepreneur Award

The recognition Sharon received validates the work Light-Core has been doing not only within the business community but in its support of the transformational change the company fosters with its clients.

Sharon remains humble with the nomination and, as a semi-finalist feels that even though she did not win, the boost of confidence she received gives her the conviction to continue on her own path of personal and professional growth.

Her market is expanding, her influence is global and she is making strides towards her mandate to work with "game changers" that effect a positive change on the world in which we live.

I've no doubt Sharon will exceed her goals and objectives by her support and due diligence in finding the right partners to duplicate her model world-wide.

Sharon's Highlights:

1) Three words of advice?
Self-awareness, Purpose and Resilience

2) Breaking barriers?
Her fear of sales and business development.

3) The most satisfying moment?
Knowing the companies she works with enjoy sustainable, profitable revenue and make a positive contribution to the global market.

Breaking Barriers / Trish Tonaj

Sharon Gilmour-Glover / Light-Core

Sharon Gilmour-Glover is an experienced consultant, speaker and teacher specializing in leadership, strategy and transformation and change management.

As an undergraduate student, Sharon underwent a teaching internship at an environmental learning centre in the United States. It was there that Sharon was introduced to the power and impact of educational programming designed using systems theory and taking a holistic approach. Soon after earning her Bachelor of Education from Brock University, Sharon began teaching business leadership programs based on the work of Stephen Covey, levering a systems approach. This early experience drove Sharon's interest in individual and team engagement, and building productivity in the workplace.

In an effort to understand what, specifically was driving the outstanding results achieved and sustained by her clients, Sharon undertook a graduate level research through a master in adult education program. Her areas of research focused on entrepreneurship, adult education and complexity theory applied across disciplines.

Sharon simplifies complex and seemingly impossible business problems by providing clients with practical, easy-to-use tools that improve their results exponentially. Sharon is the founder and Chief Implementation Officer of Light-Core. Sharon is a singer/songwriter, loves great food, great wine and great conversation.

www.light-core.com

Building An Empire – Having A Dream
The Gender Game; Does It Still Exist?
Erin Dunham – The Other Bird

As CEO of The Other Bird, Erin Dunham works in an industry that we all enjoy – food.

The Other Bird is a restaurant group that offers culinary experiences to pull people out of their comfort zone in a relaxed, easygoing way.

The names of its establishments: Rapscallion Rogue Eatery, The Alex, Two Black Sheep Snack Bar, Except for Kenneth and The Mule. They all strive to create interesting and unique dining destinations and want their patrons to be addicted to their fare to keep them coming back for more! Above all, they love preparing food that pushes their boundaries and pulls people outside their comfort zones, just a little bit. They get tremendous joy out of their business and offer menu items that you are unlikely to find at other local restaurants, such as oxtail, pig's head, stuffed saddle of rabbit and tongue 'n' cheek.

Erin started her journey in 2010 in the first location called The Alex with a rather simple corporate philosophy: "We wanted to challenge the restaurant experience in North America where most things are large-portion, low-quality. We offer small portions, high quality and no pretences." Customers agree and have been supporting her efforts ever since!

Erin has a great deal of experience in the "front of the house" and has partnered with Chef Matt who has an equal amount of experience in the "back of the house." In her words they have a "dedicated kick ass team," and have developed a formula that has contributed to their success in building an empire. "We're trying to open people's minds to new food and drink experiences and test their limits."

They have been so successful, that since the first establishment opened in 2010, they're now six restaurants strong including a boutique hotel, restaurant and banquet centre called The Arlington Hotel. This new property expands their portfolio increasing their corporate footprint within another community. This new addition to the family is in need of a little TLC and Erin and her executive team are ready for the challenge.

The previous owner gave the building a much-needed facelift, and The Other Bird will complete the project by renaming the restaurant and completing the makeover.

By incorporating their own corporate philosophy and strategically aligning its team they intend to continue to offer their unique culinary experience to the community.

Erin and her team have become so successful in defining the personality of a restaurant that they now offer consulting services to other restaurateurs, who find they are in need of a little "makeover." They provide strategic planning for the changes required to revamp a corporate strategy in order to beat the humbling odds of success.

The hospitality business, specifically restaurants, has a staggering statistic: only 2.5 per cent of those who open a restaurant cross the threshold of five years. It is a highly competitive field, where skills in business are as important as the ability to "cook great food."

Without a strong front and back of the house a restaurant is unlikely to survive and most often just one bad experience will affect the customer and have a negative impact on the bottom line.

"Hospitality" is the name of the game and Erin Dunham has grown up in the industry.

"Well, like many people who have started their own businesses, I didn't so much choose my industry as much as it chose me. I started in hospitality when I was 13. I have worked in every aspect of the business from dishwasher to cook, from bouncer to bartender, and from server to manager – throughout a variety of venues from small privately-owned fine-dining restaurants to nightclubs and high end international hotel chains. I spent most of my life being driven to get out of hospitality to be a "real" business woman. Admittedly, even when I look back on that urge to exit hospitality, I really had no idea what that other field would be. So, after I completed my undergrad in English and writing, I spent a year trying to pursue my writing career. This left me desperately unemployed until I settled for yet another job in hospitality.

It was this job in hotels that drove me to pursue my own career in the same field. I was promoted regularly and enthusiastically by my superiors, which, after a couple years, made me realize that I was working endless hours to grow an international business wherein my contribution could never really be great. This job inspired me to go back to school to do an MBA and go into the business world. While in school I met my business partner, an excellent chef, and it was an obvious progression for us to establish a business partnership.

I have ended up where I am by a series of events that have driven me to force change in my life. Most of the time, my dissatisfaction in circumstances has inspired me to find new opportunities which has most certainly resulted in my life today."

The restaurant business is very creative, fast paced and full of change. Along with the creative energy comes a passion not only for the business of food, but for people in general. Erin is a woman who pushes the boundaries by challenging business norms and creating a better environment for her company and team, which is obvious to her customers.

The Other Bird's corporate philosophy is very simple:

"To be good."

When Erin walked me through the concept she was actually sharing the recipe for her long-term success:

"We make all of our major decisions based on this simple thought. If we have to question the moral implication of any decision then the decision is to err on the side of good. I can lay out some examples for you: Charity is one aspect that is drastically different than others in hospitality. As with every business, we get multiple requests every week to donate to charity or participate in charitable events. For charity, we have a "yes" policy. If a charity asks us for assistance, we always say "yes." The only exception is if it will be detrimental to the business. For example, if we have a wedding on the same day as the event, then we would have to decline. One hundred per cent of the time we say yes to charities in our community looking for gift certificates for raffles, auctions etc.

Our policy also applies to the treatment of our co-workers. In an industry that is typically brutal to work in because of long hours and hard working conditions, we try to stand out by making decisions favourable to our entire staff. We insist that managers work reasonable hours and have safe working conditions. We provide benefits to our managers, which is most certainly not common in our industry. We try to create an environment that is safe and comfortable for everyone; part of this is to fire people immediately if they foster a negative work environment for others.

Every high-level decision that we make takes into consideration the long-term effects, both positive and negative, that it could have on our team. We always choose to do the right thing for everyone, often times to the detriment of our bottom line. – We strive "to be good."

Part of Erin's corporate philosophy includes treating people equally regardless of race, gender or ethnicity.

She has such a strong conviction that when approached by members of her community to participate in a TEDx talk, she was given carte blanche to discuss any topic. She decided to talk about the role of women in business and the issue of gender equality.

Not only did she have centre stage, but decided to address a topic that is not often discussed but identified as a big issue, primarily within the group of women in business.

She wasn't sure how it would be received by her female counterparts.

She discussed gender bias within the work place, and even used the "B" word, while citing examples within the hospitality industry and then dialed into general terms, connecting the dots through women in business.

She made the claim that women are just as responsible as men in keeping women down through our treatment of each other.

What?!

In an industry that is male dominated with, what some would consider gender roles that are divided by front/back of the house, Erin perhaps has been exposed more than most to sexism in the workplace. After all, with six brothers, she certainly has a very different personal view on conflict

Breaking Barriers / Trish Tonaj

resolution: "You pick a fight, you punch one another, someone cries and then you play transformers!" Through real life examples she is able to provide a different perspective on the subtleties that still exist within the new generation of a working team.

Erin discussed her informal "research" that, combined with her business experience, gave her a perspective that is unfortunately shared by many women in business. We congratulate colleagues who are male, and at times we seem to be jealous of the women who accomplish the same results.

She took the risk both personally and professionally and was very nervous about the outcome. Understandably, she was speaking to a room full of women!

Her resolution: Lets start with one small step and congratulate each other regardless of gender on a job well done. With this one change in attitude we can alter the course and path for future generations, who will no longer look at success from the lens of "girls" or "boys" but rather as people.

After the talk, and with great fanfare, she was approached by women of all ages, and the response was incredible. She still receives emails and messages from people, thanking her for broaching the subject. It was very well received and she is so happy she took the risk despite the fact that it brought her stress level up tremendously during the month before the talk.

x = independently organized TED event

Here is the google search: TEDx Erin Dunham or the YouTube video link: https://www.youtube.com/watch?v=TlyUX2ioEOY

Erin is very proud of the fact that she has made a positive change within her own business by crossing the lines of gender roles through the back and front of the house. She has made a conscious effort to ensure that just as many men and women are found on both sides of the business ensuring the platform is fair and equitable.

I reached out to this successful restaurateur and role model, and asked if she had any words of advice or encouragement for other entrepreneurs?

Without hesitation she replied with a mantra she applies to her own life, whether business or personal:

"Don't be shitty."

"If you have an opportunity to say something catty about someone who just walked away ... don't. If someone has said something stupid that you can jump on to highlight their mistake ... don't. If you have the chance to say something negative instead of making a small effort to make it positive instead ... don't. "Don't be shitty" applies on the small scale of our everyday behaviour and can make such a huge impact on the people around us.

"Shitty" people will NEVER be great people.

It is so easy to take the high road, yet so few people do because of habits we created from our youth: Making fun of those who are easy targets, being jealous of people instead of admiring them; not sharing in our success because we want to keep it all for ourselves, blaming others for our misfortune, etc.

Sometimes good people have bad habits. Recognizing those bad habits, especially those that are negative social reactions, and changing them to be positive reactions, will not only better other people's perception of you but, more importantly, will change your whole outlook to be more positive. "Who wants to be shitty any way?"

Erin's credo is great advice and speaks to not only her personal success but that of her company.

Taking the high road will add not only to your personal fulfillment, but to that of your team.

Every day we make a conscious choice to be good elevates the integrity of everyone we encounter throughout the day. The feeling is infectious, and leading by example is why people will support you and your business. This attitude will ultimately lead to reaching your goals and objectives.

The realization that you've achieved your goals may not always be when you open the door for business, but rather after you've made a few mistakes, experienced challenges and had to deliver on a promise to your customer.

Erin was well into the midst of her business when she realized that she had successfully "crossed the room." She owned three restaurants at the time and had reached a point where she could no longer work in the outlets because higher-level organizational duties were becoming a priority.

It was a light bulb moment when she was spending more time in the office and had to go shopping to buy additional business attire and professional clothing for events and meetings.

One day, as she was pouring over a spreadsheet she realized she had created the job she had always wanted. She, in fact, was a real life business woman. People were calling her daily for business guidance and she had the responsibility for the operations of her own company.

She was creating a management company, negotiating at regular meetings with lawyers and accountants; and had to create a management team with a focus on growing the company as a whole.

She had made the transition from caring about little projects to making major business decisions that could make or break the company.

Her light bulb moment was not when she decided to go into business but, rather, when she realized she actually had her dream job. "I was doing what I'd always done for other companies but now it was for me, and I was killing it!!"

She was realistic about the future and understanding that, without a team that shared her vision and had the ability to assist with the strategic plan, she'd never be able to sustain the growth and realize opportunities for the future.

Part of that realization, is understanding that you can't succeed without a goal, develop a team without a plan or recharge your batteries without balance. At the same time you need to combine all those ingredients with a little inspiration to challenge your creativity.

Where does Erin get her inspiration or commitment to success?

"Honestly, my greatest motivation is my team. There are so many people I work with that I know are untapped resources. There is such an incredible pool of talent within our company and I can see where they can be in one year, five years, and ten years. I am super motivated to grow our company in order to create higher-level jobs and opportunities for our current co-workers to grow with us. My motivation is to keep our employees happy and engaged, and give them the opportunities they deserve. Whether they know their potential or not, I do.

Our talented family of employees is our greatest asset. We identified this very early on, and it is a part of all of our strategy and growth plans. To be successful, we need to maintain our current employees and be very particular about who we hire, because they too need to be a part of the family we created, instead of just a number that punches in and out."

The Other Bird promotes from within so creating an environment fostering long-term growth and development is part of its work ethic and strategic plan.

As part of that recipe she also tries to strike a balance between work and play. If there is one thing that many entrepreneurs share is how the lines most certainly blur between the two.

The executive team tries to make work enjoyable by never taking themselves too seriously, which has certainly maintained Erin's sanity at times when she hasn't been able to take "time off" due to the demands of work. That being said, when she does get time off, it is relatable to the saying "work hard, play hard."

When she is at home working, her evenings are usually a mix of work and play with networking events, charity events, and other social/work events. They become more enjoyable and blur the lines with play because she often takes someone from her team.

It also helps that she would consider everyone on the executive team to be both a colleague and friend. With a healthy perspective she says, "I play a lot like I work."

Vacations are usually short trips to major cities like Montreal, Chicago, or New York where she visits all her favourite places to shop, dine, and drink.

She usually comes back more tired than when she left but always feeling rejuvenated because work was off limits. People know not to call and that her team is empowered to manage things for a couple of days until she returns. She literally disconnects from work.

The hard work pays off when you have spent the time and effort to build a team with similar goals and act quickly when you find that you need to make adjustments to the team.

One thing is for sure, nothing remains the same and keeping things fresh and up-to-date is part of the formula for long-term success.

Erin has built a team that she trusts, and her executive team has been consistent almost from the beginning. This is a true testament to her personal and business credo "to be good."

Erin's Highlights:

1) **Three words of advice?**
   "Don't be shitty"

2) **Breaking barriers?**
   Sharing her thoughts on gender bias with other female professionals.

3) **The most satisfying moment?**
   When she realized she actually had created her dream job.

Breaking Barriers / Trish Tonaj

Erin Dunham / The Other Bird

Erin Dunham was born in, lives in, and bleeds Hamilton.

As CEO of The Other Bird, Erin is one half of the creative team behind a hospitality group that includes a family of unique restaurants and a boutique hotel.

Erin has been named young entrepreneur of the year by the Hamilton and Burlington chambers of commerce, while The Other Bird received the title of outstanding mid-sized business.

She is also a painter who loves to sit back with red wine and big fat cigar.

www.theotherbird.com

Health and Wellness – Your Personal Plan
Invest In You – Your Best Asset
Trish Tonaj – Phaze2inc.

The health and wellness industry has exploded in the last 10 years with boutique gyms, training programs, spa facilities and participatory community events. Generations of individuals are becoming aware of their lifestyle choices and looking for healthy alternatives. With an aging population we are mindful of the way in which we live, work and play. Combine this self-awareness with the fact that the way we work has drastically evolved, and you begin to see a pattern for change and transformation.

I began my journey into the health and wellness industry in 2008 as a second act career. I was the president and owner of a very successful marketing company, but no longer enjoyed my work and felt it was time for a change.

The objective: Connect with executives and entrepreneurs who were not only looking for information for their personal health and wellness, but the tips and tools to reach their individual goals, and enjoy a healthy and active lifestyle.

As part of the strategy, I would include one-to-one training sessions, seminars and workshops targeted towards individuals and work teams to assist with communication and productivity. To complete the target market, keynote speaking with a focus on sharing information.

It is no secret that we live in a "gig" workforce. Many individuals work on contract with companies who offer, not only flex hours, but the opportunity to work from home, as more and more businesses become cost conscious and technology provides alternatives to the traditional model.

This flexibility creates an incubator for entrepreneurship, and many executive teams working extended hours to ensure they meet customer demands. We invest so much time into work, at times we forget about our own health. Companies have a business plan for financial success, so why not a health and wellness plan for personal success and healthy lifestyle choices? This presents a win-win strategy for everyone on the team because it benefits not only the company but the individual.

This makes perfect sense!

People are looking for an entrepreneur who will assist with the development of a personalized strategic wellness plan. Someone who understands the barriers and is able to structure a realistic individualized program, along with monitoring tools to support healthy lifestyle choices. Someone who has "walked the walk and talked the talk."

"I was an entrepreneur who was running at Mach 2 with my hair on fire, approaching burnout. I needed to take a serious look at my personal goals and how I wanted to live my life in the future."

I started the journey to become a certified personal trainer. This certificate would provide the foundation required to "information share" on health and wellness. I was pleasantly surprised to see that in order to become certified there is an education and licensing process. Attending a local community college, I completed courses in anatomy, muscle structure, nutrition, fitness options, program design and wellness theories – completing both written and practical exams, as well as first aid, to obtain certification. Annual continuing education credits and an up-to-date first aid certificate is required to renew this professional license. I chose an internationally recognized organization for certification to provide both opportunity and flexibility.

Once complete, I began an informal internship, working with other professionals to gain confidence and expertise, becoming familiar with industry best practice. This practical experience was part of my own personal criteria, which I combined with certifications. These components were part of a solid foundation for professionalism and business success.

With this information in mind, I began to work on a marketing tool that would explain my objective, provide a visual reference, and become the foundation for my new business venture.

The formula:

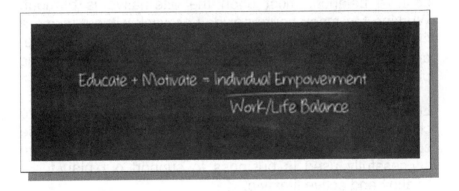

Provide health and wellness information to **educate** individuals on the choices available; include monitoring tools that will assist with **motivation** to achieve personal goals, which encourages confidence and **individual empowerment**. Once we have considered all of the options available, we are then able to implement the plan dividing our time to create **work/life balance.**

This formula is a great way to advertise to a niche market of corporate executives who have the drive, determination and discipline to be successful and apply the concepts to choosing a healthy and active lifestyle.

In theory, it all sounds so easy, but why is it so difficult?

There are a number of resources that debate the theory of work/life balance. Some feel it is completely unattainable in our current economic climate; others feel it is easy to accomplish if you have a plan. I am an advocate for living a healthy and active lifestyle, which will happen organically through lifestyle changes to encourage balance between both work and life.

As an entrepreneur or busy executive, if we don't try to achieve balance, most often the alternative is burnout. Working too many hours per day or week without taking a time out can have a negative effect, not only on family life, but our health. The best approach is to create a realistic plan that supports balance.

Life is ... unpredictable and with a personal commitment to change, then, despite life's interruptions and course corrections, we can always fall back on the skills we've successfully used in business to support our plan for a healthy and active lifestyle.

These transferable skills are often found in key performance indicators or KPIs. There are usually three qualities which define personality characteristics and provide the framework for a success strategy.

√ Drive

This personal quality is often associated with someone who has a clear focus on his or her goals and objectives. The person is willing to make the sacrifices necessary to succeed and is often open and honest in their quest to find someone they can trust to assist with the plan. These are often "Type A" personalities. They expect results and are willing to pay for the expertise.

√ Determination

This is a key factor in being able to decide if someone will be realistic enough to achieve his or her goals and yet flexible with the methods required for results.

Fitness, like business, is not an exact science and although there are many similarities to effective programs, as individuals we most often need to tweak the methods to achieve maximum results. A double-edged sword – determined to commit to a dedicated plan, but, open to various options for results.

√ Discipline

Most personal goals fail because we lack the discipline or commitment to the plan or program. We start out with the best of intensions but somewhere along the way we lose sight of our goals and begin to make choices that lead down the slippery slope to failure. When you work with individuals who have tried a program and failed – they usually have a clear, concise picture as to why it was unsuccessful and are prepared to tackle things from a different angle.

Ensuring that participants have a similar business style sets the stage for working together and describes the type of corporate executive that is both challenging and rewarding.

There is a theory widely used in business when developing goals and objectives, and is best described as the SMART Principle. This principle is considered best practice and used within the health and wellness industry to provide the roadmap for a successful program.

It outlines the framework to develop a personal plan that will ensure everyone is on the same page and working towards the same goals.

Here is the basis for the principle and how it may apply to your own plan:

The SMART Principle = Roadmap

S = Specific

Any successful plan has to have specific goals and objectives. There are many different categories you may wish to consider when developing a strategy: fitness options, nutrition tips and stress management tools. As an example, it is not enough to say that you want to lose weight. You need to define how much weight you want to lose. Perhaps you want to introduce healthy eating habits into your daily routine. A few questions would be: What kind of foods do you currently eat? What types of food do you enjoy? Or, what type of recipes are you interested in cooking? This type of questioning helps to narrow the scope to something specific, therefore meeting the criteria for your personal goals and starting the building blocks for success.

M = Measurable

Whatever goals we choose must be balanced with monitoring tools. They vary depending on the individual goal. As an example, if the goal is to introduce two servings of vegetables each day into your diet, then you must have some sort of tool that can be used to monitor daily progress. You may introduce a food diary or calendar where, the type of vegetable and serving size is written and displayed on the fridge or found on your phone or tablet. It must be something convenient, natural and easy to introduce into your daily routine. It is a visual reminder of progress and provides an opportunity to make course corrections or modifications early in the program.

Written or digital, the monitoring tools we choose set the stage for success.

A = Attainable

The goals we choose must be attainable or within reasonable reach. To use the above example, it would not be feasible to become a vegetarian; to give up meat, sugar and caffeine, feeling great and look good in one month. It is a step-by-step process that takes into consideration many different components, monitoring tools and perhaps even calling upon other industry professionals such as a dietician to assist with progress. As you can see, using the SMART principle takes a great deal of thought in order to provide a detailed roadmap to success. Attainable goals build confidence!

R = Realistic

Rome wasn't built in a day, and neither will your personal plan. Having a realistic goal that is both safe and healthy is part of the strategy. When developing the roadmap, building trust and finding the right monitoring tools will lead to success. If we fail at a goal, sometimes it is because we expected too much too soon, not because the goal was unattainable. When a realistic goal becomes a reality it will also set the stage for future growth and development, building upon one success at a time.

T = Timely

The goal cannot be so far into the future that you loose interest or find it difficult to achieve. A good rule of thumb: If you're trying to change a habit, it needs to be consistent for at least 16 weeks. If you can reach that milestone, chances are you've tweaked your routine enough to support the change in lifestyle. If you are trying to introduce a new routine, and you remain consistent for at least 28 days, you are on the path for success. Time is also on a sliding scale, as long as we define a critical path and see positive results, no one will mind if it takes an extra week or two to reach the goal.

How do you get started?

"I will never forget the day that I stood in my kitchen looking at my computer wondering if I could Google a new life? With a little chuckle, it was at that exact moment that I understood how relevant having a solid personal plan was going to be to making healthy lifestyle choices.

Change is hard work, so I literally applied the principle and began my own journey, developed a plan and began making healthy lifestyle choices."

"Who was my first customer? ME!"

I used the SMART Principle to develop a roadmap with only one goal in mind, to introduce regular exercise into my weekly routine. I developed a strategy that built confidence to achieve the goal and prove the theory. It worked!

To this day, I re-evaluate my own goals and objectives applying the principle, taking one day at a time and using the roadmap to success. Regular exercise reduced stress, increased energy and began to establish balance in my life.

One other criteria that I keep in mind when creating goals: patience.

Patience should be a quality that weaves itself into everyone's individual plan.

Living in an instantaneous society that is results driven with expectations, that you can or should be able to change in an instant, provides a lot of pressure and is not very realistic.

We certainly need patience not only with ourselves but with the methods we choose to work towards our goals.

By applying the SMART Principle, we are more likely to be successful, just by the simple fact that we've made a personal commitment to change.

Here are my three words of advice: Trust your instincts!

Develop a strong sense of self by listening to your body and reading the signs and signals as you begin the journey. Your body is an amazing machine that is connected emotionally, intellectually and spiritually to your overall success.

If you are able to trust your instincts, you will certainly be able to achieve your personal plan and transition to a place where you enjoy a healthy and active lifestyle.

The topic of work/life balance is something that touches everyone's life, and for most of us we appreciate a few tips and tools to transition through change.

In addition to work/life balance and change management tools, there are a number of topics that relate to the key disciplines introduced when I work with individuals one-to-one.

The most common topics include:

√ Fitness Options

√ Nutrition Tips

√ Stress Management Tools

√ Business Concepts & Entrepreneurship

Living a healthy and active lifestyle is important to everyone and we all need to find the time to invest in (YOU), our most important asset.

With the explosion of information on wellness and so many people exploring healthy lifestyle choices, the topic of health, fitness and change management opens the door to sharing stories and concepts for success.

There is nothing more satisfying than being able to connect with individuals and recognizing those who have found something useful that resonates with their own personal plan.

Sharing information is part of the adventure, and a great way to expand our horizons. This involves mentoring each other through the process while sharing information and expertise.

When we concentrate on an active and healthy lifestyle we organically find balance because we've made small changes or adjustments to our daily routine. They culminate into being able to divide our time between work and life.

Educate + Motivate = <u>Personal Empowerment</u>
                            Work/Life Balance

Fitness and living a healthy lifestyle is a work in progress. As we reach a goal we then begin to develop a new set of objectives that keep us motivated to move towards the balance we seek.

What is truly inspiring is that every journey is unique, every plan is individual and every challenge leads us one step closer to success.

There is a great quote from the late poet and thought leader, Maya Angelou that seems to summarize any new experience:

"Life is not measured by the number of breaths we take, but by the moments that takes our breath away."

You are your most important asset; invest in your future.

Trish's Highlights:

1) Three words of advice?
Trust your instincts!
Listen to your body and you will experience maximum results.

2) The biggest obstacle to overcome?
Finding the formula for work/life balance and starting another new business from the ground up!

3) The most satisfying moment?
When you connect with someone who experiences their own "ah ha" moment and is successful in making the changes to enjoy a healthy and active lifestyle.

Trish Tonaj / Phaze2inc.

Trish has combined her marketing and business acumen and become a Certified Personal Trainer; Nutrition/Wellness Specialist and Certified Yoga Specialist. As an advocate for assisting individuals to achieve a healthy and active lifestyle, she is a Public Speaking Ambassador, Entrepreneurial Mentor and Health and Wellness Coach.

Trish has published the book **A Diary of Change, 12 Personal Tools** where she shares her formula assisting individuals to achieve work/life balance. Her second endeavour, **Breaking Barriers, 10 Female Entrepreneurs Share Their Stories**, is a journey into mentorship, innovation and philanthropy.

As part of her commitment to working with teams, Trish has successfully completed a certificate in Mediation and Dispute Resolution from Harvard Law School - Negotiation Institute and is certified in Emotional Intelligence (Leadership, Communication and Talent Assessment) EQ-i and EQ 360 through Multi-Health Systems Inc. "Love, laugher and adventure" is her personal mantra and focus for maintaining work/life balance.

www.phaze2wellness.com

Collaboration – Like-Minded Entrepreneurs
Your Journey Begins
Karin Schuett
Circle of Life Cremation and Burial Centre Inc.

When you begin your journey, one of the most common questions you will be asked is: When was the moment you felt that "now is the time" to open your own business?

If you speak with Karin Schuett from Circle of Life Cremation and Burial Centre Inc. that day arrived after she had spent 10 years as a licensed funeral director and pre-planner. She had a very satisfying career, meeting many amazing people. Her colleagues were a source of inspiration and the families she served were always appreciative of her attention to detail, ensuring that arrangements were "just right" for their loved ones. She attributes that success to her ability to respond with empathy, kindness and non-judgment to individual requests from friends and family.

It was a collaborative effort, where the needs and wishes of many different members of a family are taken into consideration for their own celebration of life. This became the foundation for her future business opportunities.

There is no question that the landscape of funeral service has changed in the last few years, with services moving away from the traditional model: Individuals are pre-planning their own celebrations leaving detailed plans that provide their families with a sense of peace as they follow a roadmap of people's personal funeral wishes. It is a growing business and most traditional funeral homes are opening their doors to a wide variety of options that meet individual needs.

When you meet Karin, there is absolutely no doubt that she *LOVES* working with families and assisting at a time in life when most of us are overwhelmed, shocked and disoriented. Her "cooler heads prevail" approach and passion for her work is evident in her ability to provide a calm, comfortable and safe place for family members to plan a celebration of life for their loved one.

When I first met Karin, I was interested to hear how she had chosen a career in funeral service. I'd heard her mention that it is often a conversation stopper when being introduced at a party or special event. Many times she has been greeted with a puzzled expression along with the question "Did you say you are a funeral director?" followed by a shy smile or perhaps a nervous laugh.

Karin explains she was a stay-at-home Mom and the path to her chosen career was not an easy one; she was at a crossroad in her life. She was experiencing the end of a long-term marriage and had to make a decision that would provide her with not only with, an income, but fulfill a personal desire to make a meaningful contribution to her community.

She tells the story about being on a coffee date with a group of ladies in her rural community, talking about the future. They had discussed many different career options for Karin but none that seemed to fit.

As she was driving on her way home with one of her friends the words 'funeral director' popped into her mind. "That's it;" she said, "I'm going to become a funeral director." After careful consideration, she felt it was a career that would meet all of her personal and professional goals.

A few months later, with the encouragement of her friends and family, Karin enrolled at Humber College in Toronto,

Canada. As a mature mother of two, she was ready to begin her journey into a career she felt was best suited to her personality. This profession ticked off all of the boxes on her wish list, and added a few more benefits that became apparent as she completed her internship. Who knew she would be so excited to work in an industry that for most is taboo? She took her studies seriously, and after completing her mandatory internship, graduated at the top of her class.

After 2 years with a certificate in hand she began the quest to work with families in her community, moved to the big city and began a successful career.

A number of things were evident at the time in the industry:

√ most were family-owned businesses

√ family names were used to define corporate identity

√ locations within the community are often based on religious and/or ethnic backgrounds

√ there are usually two or three generations of members working in the business with men most often in management roles

√ it is a male-dominated industry

√ most services are two or three day family events

√ traditional services are held within a funeral home - offering visitation, with police escorts, limousines, church and graveside service and gatherings held at off-site locations

√ Christian services often include an evening of visitation with participation in the rosary conducted by their parish priest

√ traditional burial plots with monuments and newspaper notices

√ product selection includes traditional wooden caskets with embalming

√ funeral homes were considered the experts and information source when completing paperwork, which is often part of an aftercare program

This was a very traditional business model and throughout the years, Karin gained valuable experience becoming an efficient member of a funeral home team. Her maturity was an asset and families appreciated her calm, friendly approach.

After about five years, the industry began to change. Many family owner/operators were struggling with the challenges in the current market. Baby boomers were beginning to take an active role in their own funeral planning, cremations were becoming more popular and to meet consumer demand - Karin found her niche in a new role as a licensed funeral pre-planner.

Throughout this time of transition, management teams were finding themselves outside their comfort zone, and soon the lack of direction became an incubator for Karin to think outside the box in developing new ideas for her own custom approach.

She often found herself sitting in her office thinking of new ways to provide personalized services to this growing demographic.

At breakfast one morning, before leaving for work Karin and her partner Frank, a businessman with many years experience in the public sector began talking about offering something more to the families she served. They whispered the idea of starting their own business and felt a little uneasy at the suggestion.

In the coming months, the conversations were lengthy since there was a lot to consider. At the ages of 54 and 68 it seemed ridiculous to now open their own business and take on the financial risk of self-employment. Frank was retired and he would have to not only rethink his future but take an active role within their family-owned and operated company. Karin knew that she needed Frank's help in order to be a success. It was going to be a collaborative effort to build a team, establish a strategy, and open the doors to friends and family in their community.

They talked, researched and considered their options. After a four month period of silence, Karin decided she would not go forward with the idea. There was just too much at risk. It would be taking a huge leap of faith to leave a job that she enjoyed and carve out a very different career, despite the challenges she was facing at the office. With confidence, she decided the next day she would let Frank know she had put the idea to rest, once and for all.

She would continue working within the traditional industry, try to implement a few of her ideas and continue to receive the same sense of accomplishment from families.

But...

The next morning, as they were sitting at their kitchen table, Karin had a change of heart. She hadn't slept very well the night before mulling over the pros and cons of entrepreneurship, and all of a sudden felt it would be a mistake not to move forward. What was the worst thing that could happen? So, she took a deep breath, looked over at her husband and said, "It's now or never Frank, we are not getting any younger and I don't want to end my life wondering what if?"

Frank, needless to say, was a little startled. It had been months since they had discussed the proposal, and he too had thought they had put the idea aside – or at least on hold for the time being. Karin was so determined, and after hearing the passion in her voice, with a smile he agreed.

Frank thought: "What was the worst thing that could happen?"

They both took a second to pause, looked at each other and realized: "Oh My God! We are starting our own business!"

They figured, with Karin's funeral experience and Frank's business expertise, how could they go wrong? In a few short weeks, they put the wheels in motion.

They were going to take a chance and implement some of the new business ideas Karin had been working on for months. They began to think of a name and solidify their unique service offering. Starting a business plan, they looked for a suitable location and began to research how they would receive a license from the Board of Funeral Services.

Their corporate philosophy is to think outside the box, to not be afraid to try new things and not spend too much time worrying about what might happen in the future. Karin was aware she would be starting a business in a male-dominated industry but felt that with the change in consumer attitude, she would be able to use that to her advantage and offer a warm and feminine touch. After all, had she not been listening to her customers over the last few years who had been asking for change?

Together, Karin and Frank would develop a solid plan and work methodically through the list. Eventually, they would reach their goal, building their confidence and completing each task. When they opened the doors of their new establishment they would have created a solid foundation to succeed.

Once Karin resigned from her job, she was amazed at how many people she knew came forward to share their business expertise and sent wishes for success.

Collaborating and sharing ideas with like-minded individuals assisted with the execution of the plan.

This process was very similar to how she had started her career, working collaboratively with family members and ensuring that arrangements were "just right" for their loved ones. This would be no different, she would start her own business model by using feedback she had received from families over the last few years and offer unique personalized services.

It all began with finding the right location. They both knew how important the location would be to their success. They talked with various business owners and real estate agents to get an idea on where people felt they should be located. They plotted their competition on a map and began to mark potential sites. After visiting various options, they finally found the one that was "just right." It had once been a dance studio, so many families would be familiar with the location. As an added bonus, their landlord was a cabinet maker and offered to help, not only with space planning, but interior finishes – sourcing all of the trades required to open in record time. Next was their banker to receive financing and open a bank account, their lawyer to incorporate the name, accountant to set up the books, IT guru to develop a web site, and an insurance agent to make sure they had all the coverage required. Next, an interior decorator to assist with the colours, renovation planning and furnishings. A brand strategist discussed a strategic plan for marketing and advertising. Finally, once Karin began to go out in the community introducing herself to local business owners, she found a gift and floral designer who not only assisted with the finishing touches in decorating the space, but also offered to introduce her to some influential families within the community.

All of these industry professionals came forward to offer their advice and share their expertise, once Karin reached out and asked for assistance.

Even their banker, who was not only in favour of the project but came to visit during construction with two colleagues, asking when they wanted to expand.

Expand? They hadn't even opened the doors and the bank was offering financing for other locations within their market area.

This was too amazing!

Everyone was supportive, enthusiastic and complementary towards their unique approach. Their enthusiasm was infectious, and their ability to admit they needed the help and expertise of other professionals attracted individuals who were willing to assist throughout the project.

Karin referred to this as the domino effect. When you begin with an idea, and have the confidence and conviction to put yourself out there, amazing things will happen. Anyone who has taken that first step towards opening a business understands the many emotions that you experience as you move from one task to another, and how challenging it can be to start something from scratch – building your future. Here is a great visual: picture a set of dominos standing on end, all lined up. The beginning may represent your business idea, tip the first one over, and there you have it – they all topple over one after another in a distinct line or pattern until you've reached your goal – starting your own business!

Combine that with the day when Karin had her own light-bulb moment. She thought: WHY NOT ME?

Karin and Frank had done their homework, completing a business plan with sound financials and realistic objectives knowing that it could take almost two to three years before they would begin to see a profit and become known within the community.

Taking advice and not being afraid to ask a lot of questions is how Karin received help from so many other business owners giving her the confidence that she had made the right decision. Everyone's enthusiasm to collaborate and share expertise gave her the encouragement to continue and it confirmed that when you ask for help there is always someone available to assist.

This was collaboration at its best!

Some of her colleagues referred Karin to other business professionals who could assist with the task of opening the door, this was another domino effect, connecting like-minded individuals.

Speaking of like-minded individuals, Karin knew she was going to need at least one full-time representative. Someone who would be able to provide multiple services since she would have a limited budget. While meeting a friend for coffee, they began to discuss the qualities and personality of the ideal candidate. Karin took into consideration the skill set required, not only for this unique industry, but for a new position within a startup business. Once they began to brainstorm, she started to define and consider a job description she could use when meeting prospective candidates. She and Frank conducted informal discussions rather than formal interviews with a number of people referred to Circle of Life Funeral Home and Cremation Centre. Within a few short weeks she was introduced to someone who was the perfect fit. This individual was familiar with the industry, eager to start a new career and willing to take a chance in a new business. As an added bonus they were also interested in taking the course to become a licensed funeral pre-planner.

This was another collaborative effort!

Karin then decided she and Frank would fill in the gaps for work to be done with part-time or contract services to round out the team.

Her mantra became: "Just DO It! There is nothing worse than regret."

Karin shares this philosophy with anyone thinking of taking the plunge and starting a new venture:

"Don't pay attention to criticism, there are always negative people who don't want you to succeed. I go with the flow and always do my best. I've stopped listening to the voices from my childhood, I know who I am and what I can do."

Karin shares a personal story of her mother's comments when she revealed during a Sunday dinner that she was going to start her own company. Her mother said, "Oh my, my Karin has lost her mind." Her mom, was obviously concerned that perhaps she was taking on too much at this stage in life. Certainly, this was something both Karin and

Frank had considered. But now that Karin has realized her dream, her mother is very proud and supportive.

How long did it all take?

Well, it has been said that when you believe something is meant to be it is amazing how all of the pieces of the puzzle will come together. For Karin and Frank it happened in record time: Within four months they opened their doors to The Circle of Life Cremation and Burial Centre Inc. Before officially opening the business, they had already hosted two services and had completed two pre-need sales.

This was a great morale booster, providing the couple with the positive reinforcement they needed as they planned for their grand opening.

Karin was grateful, appreciative and euphoric that the people in her community had already begun to embrace her business and place their trust in her and the team.

The last piece of the puzzle?

Karin needed to get her name out into the community and introduce herself, her team and the services they offered. She knew she needed a robust marketing plan and a solid foundation that would give her a competitive edge at a time when people would be looking for something familiar, yet a bit different. There were some key elements to convey: trust, professionalism and integrity. Based on her past business experience Karin knew that families would only come to her if she was able to appeal to their sense of comfort, and was able to convey these three important attributes within the community.

Karin began, what some may say was an aggressive campaign. Something new for the funeral industry; most companies in the industry had been started with a "you build it and they will come" strategy. After all, funeral arrangements are not something a family member can take care of on their own. Most funeral homes see no need to advertise. With the help of her strategic marketing plan, Karin purchased newspaper ads, established a visual image through TV commercials, developed a radio jingle, offer information sessions through personal appearances in the community, hosted special events at her location and created a strong web presence to convey not only her personality but her commitment to the business.

She knew this would be expensive, but it was part of her plan for success. Her friends and colleagues became an informal focus group, offering feedback and shaping the campaign. Karin was able to establish a strong message through a visual platform and everyone on her team contributed to pulling together a cohesive strategy. This was another demonstration of the collaborative efforts of many like-minded individuals.

Karin understood that the primary message in her brand strategy was to be clear about what sets her apart from her competition. Stating her service offering would be an important key element. Inviting people to drop by and visit her location for a tour, was the "call to action." She knew that if they could experience the atmosphere she had created, that when the time came they would give her an opportunity to host their family's celebration of life.

What makes her business different?

Circle of Life Cremation and Burial Inc. not only offers traditional religious services, but also unique, non-denominational celebrations through a licensed celebrant. The celebrant meets with families and often welcomes participation through the sharing of personal memories or stories unique to their loved one. The family may also purchase keepsake gift items personalizing the experience.

These include items such as hand-made pottery urns, memorial pieces of stained glass and sterling silver jewellery. These one-of-a-kind creations feature local artists welcoming participation from the community. Artwork in acrylic, watercolour and oil found within the public spaces depict local scenery and areas of interest within the community connecting friends and family members with nature. The name of the artist is proudly displayed and featured on the web site.

In addition to a traditional casket selection, there is also bio degradable, cremation containers and one made of balsa wood where friends and family can write a personal message on the outside of the casket. This provides a unique way to memorialize the deceased person and personally connect friends and family to the experience.

As an added touch, Circle of Life Cremation and Burial Centre also offer pet memorial services under the watchful eye of Karin and Frank's pet schnauzer "Emma," who is also the business mascot. Emma greets families as they arrive which helps to convey the warmth and openness apparent when you walk in the door of the business.

Emma also appreciates the doggie treats that are available in the front reception. This wonderful addition to the team instantly conveys "we are a family too."

Throughout the first few months many visitors often asked: "Why did you choose this company name?"

On opening day, in a heartfelt speech, Frank began to describe how he and Karin brainstormed ideas at their kitchen table to come up with the name. At this time, their pet schnauzer had adopted them both and she was, of course, part of the family. If they had followed tradition the name of their business would be a combination of their surnames. Can you just imagine if they had upheld that tradition using using Schuett, Schnauzer and Schmidt or Schuett, Schmidt and Schnauzer. EEEK! Now that would be a tongue twister that even they were not prepared to tackle, when answering the phone. So, as the story goes, when they were discussing various options "Circle of Life" came to mind. They did a little research into the significance of the circle and began to realize that it was a very appropriate name for their new business.

If you Google the various definitions you'll come across a whole host of meanings for the circle as a symbol we recognize.

At the grand opening, Frank shared in his speech:

"It stands-in for God, as in 'God is a circle whose centre is everywhere and whose circumference is nowhere. As the sun, it is masculine power; as the soul and as encircling waters, it is the feminine maternal principle. It implies an idea of movement, and symbolizes the cycle of time, the perpetual motion of everything that moves, the planets' journey around the sun (the circle of the zodiac), the great rhythm of the universe.

The circle is also zero in our system of numbering, and symbolizes potential, or the embryo. It has a magical value as a protective agent ... and indicates the end of the process of individuation, of striving towards a psychic wholeness and self-realization. With the number ten, it symbolizes heaven and perfection as well as eternity."

Frank asked everyone in attendance to remember those who have gone before us, who have been personally important to us, or who have made a noteworthy contribution to our communities.

Throughout their efforts, they wanted to create a place where the healing process would begin, by offering an environment that allowed families to remember and celebrate their loved ones and their own circle of life.

The symbol alone seemed perfect for their business and Karin and Frank could not ignore the fact that it's easy to remember, recognizable within the community and in keeping with the thoughts of their banker – something that could be used at multiple locations when they were ready to expand! A culmination of great ideas once again resulted in the creation of the name for their new venture.

As part of the grand opening ceremony, Karin took the time to thank a number of people. She mentioned the names of all the individuals who had worked so hard, shared their expertise and collaborated with her and her team to create this new business.

At the end of the day it was decided that indeed it was a journey described best through the symbol of the circle, and they could not be more appreciative of all the people who had collaborated and made their dream a reality sharing in the beginnings of their very own "Circle of Life."

Karin's Highlights:

1) Three words of advice?
"Just do it" There is nothing worse than regret.

2) Breaking barriers?
Finding the courage to take the first step.

3) The most satisfying moment?
Going into work each day knowing that it's your name on the door.

Karin Schuett / Circle of Life

Karin has worked as a Licensed Funeral Director for the past 10 years after homemaking and raising a family of two – a son and a daughter. A graduate of Humber College in 2006, Karin entered the profession to express her caring, compassion and creativity.

She has worked in several locations throughout the GTA in a wide variety of roles serving bereaved families.

The many families she has served have experienced her warmth, sensitivity and practicality, as well as her concern for providing satisfying, efficient and appropriate care.

As Owner/Manager of her own funeral services establishment, Karin now offers families the benefits of her experience to provide them with a respectful, dignified and cost-effective service in the changing landscape of funeral services today.

www.circleoflifecbc.com

Marketing – Become Your Biggest Cheerleader
Build Your Personal Brand
Jennifer Kelly – New Initiatives Marketing

Jennifer Kelly is a marketing maverick with international experience, representing well-known brands in both products and services. She has worked in the world-wide market, providing both the strategic planning and execution of various concepts and theories that are ever changing in our current business climate.

Marketing is almost always the "elephant in the room." Most companies understand the value of engaging customers but find it challenging to develop a plan that will provide a solid return on investment. A lot of great ideas are left on the table in favour of the "one" concept taken to market.

New Initiatives Marketing offers services for small-to-medium businesses that don't have in-house marketing support. Jennifer Kelly is "Duct Tape Marketing" certified and able to take concepts, ideas and sales opportunities to develop a solid marketing plan with matrix for results.

It works and it sticks!

Jennifer's corporate philosophy is one shared by many entrepreneurs: "The entrepreneurial drive is really about filling a need. It is not really all that fancy, it just requires the awareness to see the need and be able to fill it with your product or service."

The development and execution of a marketing plan takes that opportunity and converts the message into sales.

Jennifer worked from 1994 to 2009 in corporate marketing roles from Toronto to Vancouver and the UK. She has worked for large brands in retail, business publishing, wireless computer networking, enterprise technology and education. She had a keen interest in international business that led her to pack her bags for Dublin, Ireland and later, London, UK to experience living and working overseas in a professional capacity. Three years abroad deepened her understanding of other cultures and international business, where she developed an appreciation for complex effective global marketing.

Jennifer admits when working for an established brand "people always returned my phone calls, with agencies and suppliers always lining up to work for us." The exposure in working with an established brand created unique opportunities when launching new products and services. Brand identity creates awareness, but with today's consumer it does not necessarily guarantee sales with profits to affect the bottom line. This practical experience was the foundation for the next chapter in her career – self-employment.

In 2009, in the large corporation where Jennifer was employed, 55 per cent of the world wide marketing team found themselves in a unique position of corporate restructuring. Although Jennifer had often thought of starting her own company she admits, "I didn't choose to start my business. It chose me."

New Initiatives Marketing was born when Jennifer realized that many companies developed brilliant strategies but lacked the resources to implement or execute the plan. Her "ah ha" moment was to take the current economic climate and provide a service to businesses that did not have a marketing department. She would offer a number of services that were flexible and transparent, giving her and her team the opportunity to develop and execute strategic plans – while analyzing various matrices for results.

She identified a need, developed a business concept to meet that need and created her own niche market.

Technology, has changed the way in which we communicate and there are always new platforms that provide creative opportunities to increase not only revenue, but customer engagement. Today's customers want a better understanding of the people behind the company, opening the doors to confusion for the solopreneur or small business. How much personal information do you want to be available as part of your strategy? Jennifer will aim to demystify the options and assist with developing a plan that includes your personality as part of your corporate image.

In addition to creative support, there are two very important marketing values that Jennifer considers for her clients. These values are as important to Jennifer as they are to her customers: People and Profit.

Jennifer ensures that messaging is sensitive to cultural, regional and generational differences and how they show up in the world, while treating people with kindness and respect. When marketing on-line the message is seen by a large audience and creating a concise message requires specific techniques and tools that engage your demographic. At the same time, clients agree that based on their mandate profit is "good." A successful marketing plan is directly related to sales, which affects the bottom line. With profit we can grow personally and professionally, reach higher goals, celebrate accomplishments and remain in business to serve the customer. The methods may have become more complex, but the objective of a marketing plan is not only to communicate values, but increase sales and revenue.

This is an old fashioned philosophy that never goes out of style!

When Jennifer opened New Initiatives Marketing it presented a unique platform to establish her brand and demonstrate the skills and expertise she acquired throughout her career by applying them to her own business.

One of the basic fundamentals: How to build a brand?

Strategically critical, many business owners are unsure and uncomfortable about how to build an image, not only for their company, but for the people who represent the company. Building a personal brand is something that evolves, starts small, building confidence and adding elements that clearly define the product and/or service to the customer. It is paralyzing for some to realize that with social media hitting "send" means the message is now as permanent and symbolic of your image as the forum is instantaneous and for some, spontaneous. To ensure the strategy has a solid foundation thoughtful consideration is given to messaging, creating a realistic budget and developing the channels for communication.

Clear, consistent and collaborative are the 3C's that define a solid strategy.

In order to build a personal brand you will be required to show up at local events, be seen in your community and have a presence online to share your experiences. Your message must be consistent with a collaborative approach, establishing relationships with other businesses in your community. A social media presence gives you extended reach when strategic partners can "like" or "share" your post within their networks. This strategy expands your target market and assists with brand identity.

What's the secret?

Information.

Relevant, interesting and thought-provoking, the content or information you choose to post or advertise will have a lasting impression on your company.

Jennifer works on developing educational information for her clients as one element in the execution of a strategic plan that attracts customers to your brand, helps them to learn from you, trust you and encourage engagement.

Jennifer developed a service directly related to content and consumer engagement called "Nimble Quotes." This is a service specifically designed for Twitter. On a subscription sales platform, inspirational and motivational quotes by famous people are tweeted on your feed as if you had sent them yourself.

Engagement is something people struggle with online "Someone liked my tweet now what?" Quotes were easily read, enjoyed by a wide target audience and a great way to start a conversation. Most important, customers began to get great results! Jennifer hired a group of researchers to begin to populate a database with positive, friendly and appropriate quotes for businesses and professionals and at the same time, connected with a program developer to create the system which is now sold as "Nimble Quotes."

The program is designed for companies that are building a brand strategy, encouraging engagement in real time. The content is positive, generic and thought-provoking, taking some of the guesswork out of the question often asked when building a presence through social media: What do I post? The service is offered monthly or annually, a 30-day trial is offered to access feedback and gauge results. Companies find the service very effective in building followers and creating a conversation.

It is a great solution for the question: What do I post?

In support of the big picture, posting information will create a platform to develop your content as a thought leader in your area of expertise. By definition, this is someone who forges new ideas – helping others understand trends, theories and concepts. It reinforces your brand and sets you apart from your competition with a unique position in the market. To build a following takes time and creates another need for content management. These techniques are part of an overall brand strategy that is highly effective but time consuming, leaving many looking for outside marketing support.

We need to concentrate on what we do best and collaborate or partner with people/companies that deliver our brand message. Who has the time in an already hectic schedule to blog or post on social media channels such as Facebook, Twitter, LinkedIn and Pinterest on a daily basis, and besides: What do I post? Jennifer has been able to identify and develop the content and platforms these opportunities provide as part of the execution of a strategic marketing plan.

Her format allows for flexibility throughout the year, depending on the type of campaign. Whether launching a new product or service, announcing an award and recognition, or simply providing information, the subscription format developed by her company meets the needs of her customer.

Jennifer's team will work on contract or retainer to provide a cost effective solution with the best platforms available to communicate the message.

The marketing plan uses the foundational elements of the Duct Tape Marketing System, Strategy – Marketing Hourglass and Content Roadmap to help build a fully developed strategy for those looking for a total package. She will explain each theory as it applies to your business and industry, establishing realistic objectives that meet your budget and criteria to convert the message into sales. Jennifer also offers marketing guidance to those who need an extra boost in strategizing their best options. This is designed to add focus to the plan and create a system to track results. All of the programs are designed to help businesses get more exposure, traction and leads. This involves taking all of the marketing efforts, tracking results and converting them into sales.

When should you consider engaging the services of an industry professional?

1. When your strategy is clear, and you now need help to execute with care and precision.
2. You need help to expertly execute your strategy for your clients.
3. You need to outsource certain marketing functions.

Here are a few questions to ask yourself as you begin to think about a marketing plan that will start the conversation for strategic direction:

Who is my customer?

What am I selling?

What is the marketing budget?

What is the value proposition?

What is my call to action?

How do I communicate the message?

How do I create raving fans?

These questions will begin a dialogue that will shape and form your plan, and develop the matrix for results.

As basic as it may seem, Jennifer has practical advice for developing the cheerleader in all of us and giving us a head start on corporate messaging:

"Being your own cheerleader really starts with you believing in what you do and going for it. Whatever you need to do to get your mindset right, invest in that to get you started."

As part of the dialogue and waving your own pom-poms:

"There will be good days, bad days and great days. You will need the resilience to be able to celebrate the highs, learn from the lows and celebrate when things are great. When you believe in yourself and what you do then you will find the ways to best communicate your message. Looking for a strategic partner in marketing is no different than connecting with a lawyer or accountant. You pay for the expertise and connect with someone who understands both you and your business."

Her words of advice for any business owner:

"Go For It".

"You just never know what you can do or where your limits are until you try. In all of my challenges in life – moving overseas with $700 to start a fantastic life in Dublin, then moving to London, starting my own business and developing a social media service, there has been a common theme. Everything that I was fearful of either never happened or, if it did, was barely a blip on the radar screen and easily dealt with. If I hadn't tried, I would never be able to appreciate the success."

We can spend too much time analyzing and allowing the fear of making a mistake dampen our enthusiasm.

There are always options and opportunities that provide a solution to any problem.

A test pilot is a great way to create a customer profile and begin to build a strategy. The results will give you a foundation for building your brand based on your ability to analyze the facts and gauge the response from your customer.

Fear is the one thing that Jennifer feels every entrepreneur faces at one time or another, and being able to tackle that obstacle head on gives you the ability to overcome the emotion, building confidence and permission to enjoy your success.

Working with her clients combined with her own experience Jennifer has come to realize that "you will be challenged to raise your game in several areas and get out of your comfort zone more often than you may like, but you can still be you.

Entrepreneurship will just push you to become the best version of you on the way to serving your clients with more of your talents."

One of the things that Jennifer personally had to overcome was her fear of sales. She knew that if she wanted to grow her business she needed to reach more people, selling and closing deals.

She began to take training courses to learn new techniques and build confidence. Once she had the initial skills under her belt she lost the fear.

Refining her skills gave her the ability to accept that the sales process would be a life-long training session.

When she began to embrace the fear there were so many additional opportunities.

Opportunities build sound strategies and create innovative ideas and practical campaigns.

Take an online audit to see if you have all of the pieces of the puzzle to begin your marketing success journey.

>   https://newinitiativesmarketing.com/your-audit/

You will answer questions in the following categories:

Business Category

Ideal Customer

Competition

Platforms to educate and promote

Advertising Vehicles to Build Trust

WWW - World Wide Website

Lead Generation and Sales

Keeping Score

As an entrepreneur answering this questionnaire will make you think outside the box, analyzing your own business and creating an opportunity to think about formalizing or changing your own marketing plan.

For Jennifer, this online tool assists with qualifying potential customers and the opportunity to achieve her sales goal of reaching more people and closing more deals.

Jennifer has been able to build her own brand by putting her skills and expertise into practice through New Initiatives Marketing.

Building confidence with her customers who understand the value of her company's products and services is what builds long-term business relationships.

The referrals received through happy customers who've received results is a great way to build a brand and is a wonderful complement.

"Go for it." What have you got to lose?

Jennifer has become her own cheerleader in building a brand with the tape and it sticks!

Jennifer's Highlights:

1) **Three words of advice?**
   "Go for it"

2) **Breaking barriers?**
   When she realized her business experience provided an opportunity to meet the needs of her customers by offering a marketing solution.

3) **The most satisfying moment?**
   Being paid for her expertise.

Jennifer Kelly / New Initiatives Marketing

Since 2009, Jennifer Kelly has run her own company, New Initiatives Marketing (NIM). The focus is on partnering with clients to implement and execute effective marketing strategies. Some call it marketing project management, other clients refer to them as "quarterbacking all our marketing stuff."

Jen recently created, developed and launched a Twitter inspirational quotes service called Nimble Quotes (nimblequotes.com). This service posts inspirational and motivational quotes to subscribers Twitter accounts as if they've tweeted the quotes themselves. We can't talk business all the time, so quotes can be a way to connect emotionally with an online audience you are trying to build rapport with.

Prior to starting her company, Jen spent 17 years in the marketing departments at big brands such as the Financial Times UK, Siemens and Motorola. A keen interest in international business led her to pack her bags for Dublin, Ireland and later, London, UK to experience living and working overseas in a professional capacity. Three years abroad deepened her understanding of other cultures, international business and an appreciation for how complex effective global marketing can be. Jen was part of the leadership team to bring the first TEDxWomen event to Toronto in 2013.

www.newinitiativesmarketing.com

Lifestyle Choices – A Balancing Act
Your Family In Business
Odile, Kinza and Gabrielle Nasri - ça va de soi

ça va de soi offers both manufacturing and retail sales of high quality knitwear. Family-owned and operated, the retail division began in 1989, and the company has six stores in Montreal, Quebec City, Ottawa and Toronto.

Their corporate mission: "Bring the best materials from Italy and Egypt, assemble with top-notch spinning techniques and craftsmanship to deliver a product that survives trends."

When you meet the matriarch, Odile Bougain Nasri, CEO, retail creative director, she will happily say that the notion for the business was developed in conversations "at my kitchen table." Her husband Antoine was in the garment business and when the wholesale landscape began to change they decided to open their first retail store. "I had no experience in retail at all but passionately believed there was a customer for high-quality knitwear."

In order to establish their brand, they kept both the wholesale division and their first store operating in tandem until they had built a foundation to become exclusive with their unique brand.

ça va de soi, French for "It Goes Without Saying," has been built on a "couture fashion" model. The company offers a timeless, permanent collection with seasonal fashion lines that complement the current selection twice per year. The business model is organic in both product and service and has been a consistent part of the corporate strategy. The family strives to ensure that the stores become part of the local community and they have chosen street-front locations to be able to interact with their clientele and provide personalized service. The stores were designed by Montreal architect Philip Hazan, who enacted the family vision to transform the space into an atmosphere that is both warm and inviting. Upon entering their stores, a library feeling at each location greets the customer in an atmosphere that's both traditional and contemporary.

One of the many unique features: old European black and white movies play in each location for all to enjoy. This is a charming touch that feels familiar and creates a warm, cozy atmosphere. Mr. Hazan completes the look with organic materials through the selection of wood, marble and stone, which connects with the natural fabrics.

The team not only offers customers comfortable, timeless clothes, but information on the various types of wool, cotton and cashmere used in manufacturing. As an added bonus, detailed instructions on caring for the fabrics are discussed including a selection of private label laundry soaps so that your favourite garments will be enjoyed for many years.

A personal commitment to quality, price and style is guaranteed with a "we NEVER go on sale" policy, which is refreshing and appreciated by customers.

A recent addition for busy women on the go is the *ça va bain* laundry service "Stop-and-Drop" that is offered to customers with an in-house store facility in Montreal.

With a smile, Odile tells a story about working with her sales team in the early days of the business when a certain member of her team felt that no one would be interested in hearing about how the product was made. After a few weeks of working in the store, she was soon asking Odile for additional tips and manufacturing techniques that she could explain to customers – so much for no one being interested in the "how to" of fashionable knitwear!

This confirmed the concept and was the beginning of a solid niche market!

As part of the commitment to quality, the company manufactures its own designs, providing a competitive edge and connecting customers with its organic philosophy. International in scope, their strategic partnerships have been established in Canada, Italy and China. With an investment in the future and a commitment to the finest details and craftsmanship, the family has developed a brand that provides both style and fashion in knitwear.

This is truly a family committed to the business, each with an area of expertise that relies on the efforts of one another for success.

Odile continues to oversee the retail division with her vision in both marketing and communications. The stores have been featured in many local newspapers and magazines as both fashionable and innovative. As the matriarch, she is warm, inviting, and her enthusiasm is infectious.

Working as part of her team, she understands the concept of succession planning and has welcomed the addition of her two daughters into the business. Each daughter has her own area of interest and the opportunity to influence the company through their individual personalities while complementing and supporting each other for continued growth. University educated, part of the mandate was to expand their business theory and develop their work ethic. With a "sink or swim" attitude the girls joined the company. They welcomed the challenge and bring a fresh, new perspective to the business.

Kinza is completing an apprenticeship of sorts in manufacturing and her personal sense of style appeals to a modern customer and relaxed lifestyle. Her younger sister,

Gabrielle, is taking the reins in operations and working with the team of committed individuals who work "front line" with the customers and convey the *ça va de soi* commitment to excellence in service.

The company's corporate philosophy is best described through three words:

1) **Organic** in both environment and product

2) **Progressive** through the types of yarn and display of the merchandise

3) **Timeless** with their permanent collection which can be worn for many years, layered with seasonal fashion colours with accessories.

As a customer, I can say with conviction that the positive energy you feel when you meet the Nasri family is indeed found in the stores, and experienced through the warm and cozy atmosphere created by the team.

The family has built its brand and accomplished its mission with a commitment to continued success. There is a strategic plan for growth and a vision for the development of new and innovative products.

If you ask Odile, she will say that the children have been part of the business from a very young age. Not only working in the summer, during school breaks and on weekends, but also contributing to the many family discussions. She is very grateful that the family and business have been able to work together for many years.

"The children have been exposed to an entrepreneurial lifestyle and are very aware of what's involved when working as a family in business." She says they understand both the risk and reward with self employment and have a very strong appreciation for the lifestyle they have enjoyed.

Lifestyle is very important to their family and working together has given them a unique appreciation for their individual approach to enjoyment in life. Working long hours has brought the family closer together and yet at the same time created a mutual respect for their individualism. This is also true for the merchandise, which provides individuals with a casual, classic look you can personalize.

The family members and staff have had the pleasure of establishing relationships with many generations of customers. There have been times when mother, daughter and granddaughter are all wearing different styles, colours and designs from the line – a compliment to the family's notion that lifestyle plays a role in how people dress and the clothes we wear are both emotional and personal.

The versatility of their classic designs allows for the expression of each individual. Whether classic, modern, casual or sophisticated, *ça va de soi* offers a sense of style and appeal to a discerning customer, who can imprint their own personality into the clothes. The team is pleased to contribute to the "joie de vivre" of so many great ladies.

"Passion" is a word that best describes the family's connection to the business. Each member of the family has a vision that demonstrates a commitment to their area of expertise, which they recognize is woven together and contributes to their overall success.

Odile manages brand identity, coordinating all of the departments, ensuring they work together with a strong connection with the customer. As a big picture thinker, she uses her instincts to smooth the rough edges that at times occur not only between family members but the team.

She constantly reminds everyone that the customer experience is the most important consideration.

Kinza, the artistic director will say that her father has *ça va de soi* tattooed on his heart and everything he does reflects a commitment to quality, style and innovation. Purchasing inventory approx. 10 to 12 months in advance of the season means that everyone's input is welcome and required in order for the manufacturing team to choose the right colours, designs and fabrics for the next season.

She is working towards developing a working knowledge of the various techniques used throughout the manufacturing process and intends to build on the commitment to quality and design for the future.

Establishing relationships and strategic partnerships with not only the factories, but the artisans who work on the garments, is part of her mandate.

Gabrielle, the director of sales and operations, believes that the retail division is a work in progress, as the team changes and grows organically through time. Her leadership style assists each member of the team to become part of the family. She is always learning new concepts and business techniques to ensure that everyone on the team is current and informed. She is not afraid to admit that she has made mistakes, and her honesty and commitment is appreciated by everyone, who becomes a brand ambassador.

"Passion" and "heart" are qualities they look for in every employee, and these must be evident throughout the interview process with all new members of the team.

The organizational chart confirms a commitment to a family atmosphere with open lines of communication. The spirit and feeling of belonging as part of the family has many possibilities for the team to grow and prosper, as the company expands.

As a visionary, Odile's three words of advice would be: "follow your instincts." "We would never have started the business if we had simply taken into consideration market conditions, the changes in economic climate and the fashion business in general."

"Dreams create the foundation for success."

Odile will be the first to admit that running a business has not been easy, you have to make many sacrifices but in the end it has been worth it. Without hesitation she admits that she would not change one thing. All of the experience – good and bad – has had a positive effect on the family in business, giving them the courage and confidence to enjoy and experience "life."

As an entrepreneur, at the beginning of the journey to start the business Odile can remember the biggest obstacle was capital investment.

The family members started the business with a concept backed with practical knowledge. They needed to build a brand and retail presence based on quality, value and design. Once they had begun to establish brand identity, this created a foundation for careful and strategic expansion. The additional stores have been in response to consumer demand, and the ability to connect with the community in each market.

As part of recent expansion plans, Kinza took on the project of introducing an online, e-commerce store in June of 2015. Now, she has enough data to allow online purchases, which will appeal to a wide demographic. Their mandate is to create a similar customer experience as the one found in the stores, providing individual service and the opportunity for customers to connect with the brand through social media. This has been a huge undertaking and as part of the strategy, the family postponed the opening of another store in Toronto, instead devoting the time and energy required to maintain brand integrity while venturing into the new sales frontier. The family is firm in their commitment to continue with the development of the online store because of the obvious sales potential. The motivating force is to be able to reach customers looking, not only for knitwear, but quality merchandise within their couture model.

Creativity is part of the leadership team's values. Each team member contributes to the style, design and fabrics chosen for each season. As with any creative business each team member's personal inspiration supports their individuality and each member of the team enjoys similar characteristics.

Odile refers to a family friend, her adopted grandfather, "Joe," who was an entrepreneur and self-made man, successful by anyone's standards. She admired his positive energy and ability to enjoy life. Odile fondly recalls instances where Joe overcame obstacles and not only enhanced his life but that of his family. His commitment to both family and business are a constant inspiration for Odile to follow her dreams.

Kinza looks to the famous couturier Coco Chanel. Coco began her business by manufacturing and selling hats and later expanding into knitwear. A traditional couturier, Chanel later modernized ready-to-wear fashion, encouraging women to express their individuality through their clothes while maintaining standards of quality and design. Chanel and her success story provide continued inspiration to Kinza in her role in design and manufacturing.

Gabrielle is the free sprit of the group, finding inspiration from the people she meets in day-to-day life. She connects with the human spirit and stories shared by customers. This enthusiasm fuels her energy when managing the ever-expanding sales team. For the family, this creative energy and inspiration is celebrated in the freedom to make the choices necessary for its continued growth, both personally and professionally.

The connection to the family's lifestyle is directly related to its corporate philosophy, and the Nasri family lives by three simple words: organic, progressive and timeless.

Organically through time, the team's business experience has provided them with the ability to make lifestyle choices that offer freedom and directly connect back to the family in business. The street-front locations give them flexibility with store hours, and, by working as a management team, they experience trust, judgment and creativity. As a family, they individually appreciate each other's skills and expertise and each welcomes the challenges that contribute collectively to the company's continued success.

The Nasris are a family that is responsible, appreciative and respectful of the opportunity to work together, doing what they love. Who doesn't want to live their dream?

Odile, Kinza and Gabrielle's Highlights:

1) **Three words of advice?**
   "Follow Your Instincts"

2) **Breaking barriers?**
   Finding the capital investment to expand logically, organically and strategically.

3) **The most satisfying moment?**
   Dreams create the foundation for success.

Kinza, Odile and Gabrielle Nasri / *ça va de soi*

Knits are in our Nature

Since 1972, *ça va de soi* has taken the time to make knits part of our very nature. We've taken the time to choose our fibres carefully: the finest soft and warm wools from faraway lands, and the rarest Egyptian cottons that bear the name of the soil that witnessed them grow.

We've taken the time to meet master spinners from Italy — the best in the world — who give body, elegance and colour to the raw materials. The time to do things well and to pay attention to the imperceptible details that transform clothing from simple to unique. The time to observe how women move, so we can create pieces that move with them from morning to night and eliminate the boundaries between seasons, eras and generations.

For several years, *ça va de soi* founders Antoine Nasri and Odile Bougain Nasri have also taken the time to pass their unique know-how on to their children, turning knitwear into a wonderful family affair.

www.cavadesoi.com

Financial Wellbeing – Creating A Workbook
Organizing Your Financial Statement
Lee Helkie
Helkie Financial & Insurance Services Inc.

Success comes in many different shapes and forms. It means different things to different people, and everyone throughout his or her lifetime enjoys the feeling of success.

One element of business is universal – financial success. Having the money to buy your first car, condo, house or simply go on vacation is important to everyone. So what do you do when your business is successful and you're now ready to plan for your future?

Of course, before we even think about the future, we need to ensure we are able to maintain a certain standard of living for ourselves and our families.

The necessities of life are at the top of the list and we've all heard and read stories about individuals, regardless of their financial wealth, planning for the future.

As an entrepreneur, or solopreneur we need to leave ourselves with a something for a rainy day. The little bit of assurance that we have money tucked away "just in case."

Our financial plan or workbook will give us the opportunity to build on our financial success, and plan for our present and future needs and wants. So how do we begin to think about our finances both personal and professional?

When speaking with Lee, she has a very simple theory:

"Start with adding up what you own and subtract what you owe. Then think about what you spend and what you make. We need to make sure those numbers are healthy. If not, then you know where to start to make adjustments."

When Lee was in university the author of the Wealthy Barber, Dave Chilton was a guest speaker and what he had to say 25 years ago is still relevant today:

Pay yourself first!

"If not you – then who is going to take care of you?"

What better place to begin than at the beginning. All entrepreneurs start with a financial goal in mind. They have a story about how they got started in business that sets the stage for their future and begins the roadmap for their own financial success. It is important to create your financial workbook and plan for the future at the beginning of your career. This foundation will build a solid future with a strong financial statement. A rule of thumb is to take 10 per cent of what you earn and begin to invest. This may be difficult to do at the beginning of a business venture, and the formulas vary, depending on who you choose to assist with your plan, but, the theory remains the same. We need to save for our financial security.

Finding the right partner when planning for the future is as important as having the money to invest. This is serious stuff and something most of us don't typically enjoy. When we begin to save we usually have a little less disposable income to spend on what we enjoy. It is a paradox: You can have a certain amount to spend now, or save a little to spend later! It is not exactly "fun" and finding someone who understands the fine line between saving and spending is very important when we plan our financial future.

Lee Helkie is both an insurance agent and financial planner who began her business career in her teens, working for a family friend in retail. She cut her teeth in the world of business through the influence, trust and opportunity presented to her by her parents when she was only 16. Understanding the value of money at an early age was something she learned early on and her journey began with her first pay cheque.

It wasn't long before she began to work in the insurance industry, following in her father's footsteps and establishing a resume working part-time throughout university. She had no idea how important this practical knowledge and work experience would be in her own career. When she began looking for a job, it was during a recession and her practical work experience gave her the competitive advantage over her classmates. She was able to secure a job upon graduation. When employers took a look at her resume, it not only conveyed experience, but the energy and interest to invest in her and her future.

"I always had an eye for business and was unwittingly influenced by my father, who spent his career in the insurance business. My first real job was at an insurance company where I was given a lot of leeway to make sales in my own way. I really liked the client interaction. More importantly, I felt a passion for what I was doing. Helping people plan and protect themselves and their families. From early on I wanted to work for myself. Or shall I say, for my clients. I saw great value in the work of a good advisor. I was eager, and because of my enthusiasm was invited to many client meetings to observe and absorb all they had to teach. As a result, I had many advisors asking me to join their practice. In my heart, I knew I could never join someone else and that I wanted to work for myself."

The seed of entrepreneurship was sown.

After university, Lee decided to continue to build her resume within the insurance and finance industry, working for large companies. She felt in order to have well-rounded experience she had to see both sides of the fence. Not only working with the customer but working with those who worked with the customer! It was a great opportunity to expand her industry experience and build her knowledge and expertise.

It was a solid plan with a good future, but eventually she did make the decision into the world of entrepreneurship.

After a satisfying and interesting career that spanned more than fifteen years, Lee found herself working for a large company in a senior management role. She had learned a great deal but was looking for a new challenge. Her husband had started his own financial and insurance agency and as she was raising her family decided that she'd start a new division of his company. She made the decision to become an entrepreneur within the structure of a successful business and joined the firm in finance and insurance while exploring a new revenue stream: group benefits.

Lee had traveled full circle and was now following in her father's footsteps and working on-on-one with individuals and their employees to plan for the future.

It was the right decision at the right time in her career.

What Lee didn't expect was how difficult it was to transition into entrepreneurship.

There is so much more to a successful business than providing excellent customer service and advice to clients. She had to practice what she preached and focus the planning expertise she gave her clients on her own business. The decisions she made would provide her and her husband with the financial success they needed for their own family – a charming turn of events.

Within the first year she soon realized there were three key components to entrepreneurial operations:

1) Systems
2) Delegating
3) Teamwork

Systems
Having the right systems in place gives everyone on the team a roadmap to not only "how" to do business, but how to interact and build relationships with customers. Whether an informal process or part of their strategic business plan, having the right systems builds confidence for everyone on the team.

Delegating
Lee will be the first to admit that "letting go" and being able to delegate tasks to her capable team has been a challenge. What she realized was that delegating gave her the time she needed to do the things she enjoys and that provides income for the business. When looking at our "to do" list sometimes it just feels that we can get the jobs done faster without having to bother someone else and take the time to explain the details. In fact, the opposite is true, empowering the team can actually increase everyone's productivity!

Teamwork
Hiring individuals who believe in your corporate philosophy and uphold the values of the company is paramount to your overall success. Working together makes the team stronger and business healthier. The workplace environment conveys commitment to both your clients and each other creating a collaborative, relaxed atmosphere.

When Lee begins to work with a new client the most important thing is to begin to build a rapport with building blocks for a long-term relationship. She keeps in mind that for most people this is not a "feel good" purchase. We all know that we need to buy insurance and save for the future but no one wants to commit the money!

In order to try and change the experience from negative to positive, Lee begins by discussing her client's wish list. This begins the process of establishing a sound plan that speaks to their individual needs and wants.

They focus on goals and she often asks: "Where do you see yourself in the future?" Along the way, they weave the "What Ifs" into the conversation, which allows her to discuss the features and benefits of a contingency plan that will affect their financial statement. Lee's philosophy is to build a road map that is both realistic and fluid, taking steps that will lead to a clients ultimate goals. After all, life is busy, goals may change through time and providing options is what establishes a long-term client relationship and builds trust.

It should be fun and empowering to take control of your personal situation. What is important to remember is that YOU are in control of the plan and YOU can adjust the plan based on your circumstances. Lee finds this chart helps clients visualize the different stages of their lives and understand forward planning is required to be successful.

As part of the process, Lee uses a graphic to outline life's journey, and demonstrates our needs and wants in chart form, throughout various stages in life. For those who are visual, it's a great chart that starts conversation and begins a dialogue towards what will ultimately be a customized plan for each individual and his or her company.

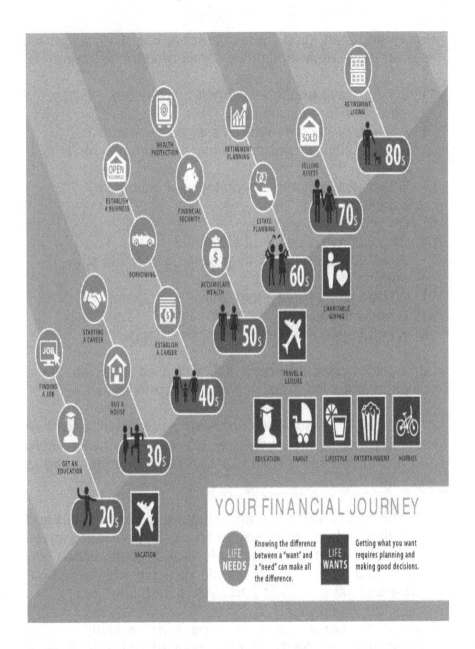

Over the years, Lee has noticed that too many people look at planning their finances as scary or overwhelming. What's helpful? Think of it more as a financial health check. You're just making sure all of the moving parts are working.

Before you start, give yourself a score out of 10, and then, re-score yourself when you've considered the following:

1) Do you have enough savings to cover your expenses for four months?
2) Are you protected in the event you can't work?
3) Is your family protected if you don't come home tonight?
4) Do you have money saved for your children's education?
5) Do you have a will?
6) Do you have a power of attorney?
7) What does your ideal life look like when you stop working?
8) What age do you want to retire?
9) When will you sell your business?
10) What do you need to do to make it happen?

For a more detailed check list, visit Lee's website for a complementary download for your own reference.

It really is all about your goals and objectives and then working towards those goals. YOU are planning your future and giving yourself a roadmap to financial freedom and to enjoy life!

The risk and reward for entrepreneurship doesn't start and end with your business – you need a solid plan that weaves together both personal and professional goals. When you review your financial statement, you may combine both numbers to get a realistic perspective on the future.

Throughout Lee's years of experience working with a diverse group of clients, she has noticed that regardless of profession we are all quite similar.

There seem to be three areas that we often don't consider when developing a roadmap for success:

1) We work for our customers, perhaps our companies, but rarely for ourselves.
2) We forget that not having a guide or roadmap leaves our families at a disadvantage.
3) We rarely think about the "big picture" and often get caught in the details creating confusion.

We all need to take a balanced approach. Lee and her team recognize that you can't always think about the future. You need to live for today. What's important is that you have a game plan for both, as part of one cohesive plan. They understand that even when you have a plan, things can change and you may need to adjust your plan based on current circumstances. When you work with an advisor who understands both the industry and business, you have a relationship with someone who can walk you through options to realize your goals and objectives.

As a trusted partner in your success, Lee will give you alternatives to consider when making adjustments or corrections to the plan. She'll often reflect back to the beginning to discuss basics of the relatively simple formula:

1) How much do you own versus how much do you owe?
2) What have you saved?
3) How much do you think you will need to retire?

Then do the math at a reasonable rate of return, trying to incorporate taxes if you can, and ultimately summarize the formula. One of the important to remember is that like you Lee is implementing a plan that is fluid and at times needs to change. Her personal approach is much the same as those of her clients. "Walk the walk, and talk the talk." As an entrepreneur, she shares one of the things she finds challenging and often her clients agree that the number of choices can be overwhelming.

"Choices – we have so many choices about the way we do business, what business we are in, and who we deal with. It can be overwhelming at times. But it is our choice. We have the power and control to make those decisions. The hard part is doing it. What I always remember is that You have to be brave, believe in yourself and persevere. What I often share is that it isn't easy for me either! Fear is a powerful enemy and it can hold you back. I have gotten the same answer from every successful person I know: Success takes time. It never happens overnight. I try to keep that in my mind when I doubt myself or my ideas, as I work though my own plan. As with my clients, I have to work hard at it. I also agree that no one ever sees the hard work, just the rewards. As an entrepreneur, I experience the same options, choices and decisions. Your company's direction and success is based your decisions. There is no safety net unless you have a roadmap and plan for the future. You succeed or fail based on your ability to stick to the plan and make adjustments through time. I often remind myself that with choices come both responsibility and consequences. There are no short cuts to working hard and I share the same decisions in my own business."

That is perhaps why Lee's clients have a friendly connection with her as their advisor. She is realistic and honest in her approach when planning for the future, making it feel a little less scary and injecting a little more fun. She often shares these three words of advice:

Brave – Be brave. No matter what you can handle it!
Persevere – Nothing in life worth having comes easily.
Believe – If you don't believe in yourself, how can others?

As part of her own success journey Lee will share stories about her experience on the topic of entrepreneurship from a female point of view: "Women are very hard on themselves and I'm in that club. I feel I've lived a lifetime in the last five years. I've had to dig really deep inside myself to find strength and confidence. I have learned a lot about who I am. I am stronger than I thought, I am more controlling than I thought, but, I am also weaker at times too. I have learned to let myself be. You need to let go, to be weak and vulnerable, and to then be strong and confident. Nobody has it all together all the time. In this business, trust is a big part of who and what I am. What I've come to realize is that this is my life. I made the right decisions and I'm exactly where I should be with my business, going in the right direction."

The message she shares with all businesses as part of her corporate strategy:

"Saving for yourself gives you options no matter what life throws your way. What we have to keep in mind is that we always have choices. When we have a solid plan, at least we can affect the outcome.

"You have one life to live – do it well."

Lee's Highlights:

1) **Three words of advice?**
   Brave,
   Persevere,
   Believe

2) **Breaking Barriers?**
   Overcoming the fear of entrepreneurship.

3) **The most satisfying moment?**
   Understanding that having "choices" gives you freedom.

Breaking Barriers / Trish Tonaj

Lee Helkie / Helkie Financial & Insurance Services Inc.

Lee, one of Canada's **"50 Women of Influence"** in the Life Insurance Industry, has spent her career on both sides of the fence, both corporate and as an advisor. She has worked with and in many practices seeing what is working and how to do things better. After graduating from the University of Waterloo, she began her career with one of Canada's largest insurance companies. She held Management positions in multiple product lines working with some of the Industry's Top Advisors. She chose to leave that career and join her husband Jim in building Helkie Financial & Insurance Services Inc. to follow her a passion of helping Canadians make informed choices about their finances.

Lee has appeared in several radio, newspaper, magazine, and television articles covering a wide variety of Financial Planning, business and family topics. She regularly speaks at Public Events and conferences. Her journey has been one of personal growth and discovery. She shares that with her clients and colleagues, adding a deeper value to their relationship.

www.helkiefinancial.com

The Art of Reinvention:
Turning Lemons Into Lemonade
The Power of Positive Energy
Gloria MacDonald – Life Alchemy Inc.

If there is one thing to be certain of, everyone, and I mean everyone, has a story. Nothing in life happens by chance and very few go through life without the hands of time reaching out with both opportunities and challenges along the way.

In our youth we may make mistakes that provide us with the moments that shape and form who we are and where we are supposed to be laying the foundation for future growth with a database to learn from our mistakes. It may be when you go to college or university, begin a career, find a life partner, start a family, open a business or retire. No matter when life's lessons present themselves, if you are at all a fatalist then you will believe that these are moments in time when we are supposed to learn one of life's lessons and continue along the journey.

What is interesting is how we perceive and receive the opportunities, so that the challenges are a little less onerous and the path becomes a little easier or smoother, as we transition from one lesson to another.

When I met Gloria, I was taken with her sense of positive energy, contentment and commitment to be the very best "Gloria." I had made a connection through LinkedIn and a personal recommendation from a friend to contact her about this book.

I had Googled her business to get a sense of where and what type of services she offered, but had no idea of the history or story behind this amazing lady, and her personal and professional journey.

We met at her condo in Toronto; very graciously she welcomed me into her home and I remember thinking, *"I'm a perfect stranger having only talked on the phone as a form of introduction and yet here she is inviting me into her personal space to meet and discuss my project."* She offered to make lunch and I brought along a small bottle of Veuve Cliequot contributing to the special occasion and giving us the opportunity to toast our new success journey.

We talked about her skills and experience and how sharing her story would be a great contribution to the book. She is a certified "Dream Builder" coach and "Life Mastery" consultant through the Life Mastery Institute in California, and is committed to sharing her knowledge and experiences. Gloria hosted her own weekly TV and radio shown, and has been featured in numerous national newspapers and magazines. She has more than 20 years experience, and is also an international speaker, educator, motivator, and author. With clients in Australia, Germany, Chile, Mexico, and the UK as well as all over North America, including New York, Boston, Toronto, Chicago, Vancouver, Portland, San Francisco, Los Angeles and Honolulu – she has a diverse and robust business.

I was intrigued and impressed with her credentials, so, I asked her to tell me a little about her journey. She said: "I had a very successful, highly personalized matchmaking business, called Perfect Partners, for 14 years. During the 14 years in business, we introduced more than 8,500 couples. We had many successes and numerous marriages. The match-making business is very personal, with lots and lots of variables and intangibles, and it can be highly emotionally charged. It is impossible to predict chemistry and guarantee success in finding love, or a long-term partner or marriage for every client.

One client, where we hadn't been successful, was of course dissatisfied. Despite offering a refund for services that had not been rendered, she posted a comment on a consumer review website.

The Internet is a very powerful tool.

This one review literally caused the business to go from thriving one month to absolutely no business or revenue the next. It was as if a tap had just been shut off. The phone didn't ring and there were no emails.

Over the course of three months, with zero revenue and significant expenses, I made the very difficult decision to wind the business down. We could not just shut down overnight because, although we had no new clients, we still needed to honour our contracts and work with our existing clients.

This was extremely challenging both personally and professionally.

The timing, on the other hand, was very interesting because I had been giving serious thought to making a career change, and wondering what I could do that would inspire and motivate me again. After all of those years as a matchmaker, I was tired and wanted to find something new. Now, with the clarity of hindsight, I see exactly how I, energetically and unconsciously, co-created the downfall of my own business.

While working with our Perfect Partners clients I saw so clearly how, if individuals were open to it, I could show someone how to shift their energy and get very different results – the results they were looking for in dating.

I realized that inspiring, motivating and teaching people, thereby empowering them to discover and create a life they loved living, in all areas, was what I was passionate about. From this, the idea came to me to coach people on how to shift their energy and create their lives intentionally, by design rather than by default.

It was at this time that Life Alchemy was born."

Gloria had not only been through a difficult transition professionally but she had found a way to turn "lemons into lemonade." Taking a series of events or circumstances and being able to see an opportunity for the future.

As with every transition there was a catalyst for change and a reason for the energy shift. Gloria went on to share the exact time she experienced her "ah ha" moment: "I was at a seminar in Phoenix, Arizona, about three weeks after I realized that Perfect Partners was falling apart. I questioned whether or not I should have come to the seminar, because my financial situation was so bleak. I was going through a very "dark night of the soul." I was in a deep state of despair and I felt like a walking zombie. My energy was extremely low.

One of the speakers told his story of success and how he had come out of near bankruptcy. There was a crack and a glimmer of light that came through as he shared his story. I experienced a very tangible shift in my own energy, as if a cloud just lifted and the heavy, heavy fog was gone. At that time, I didn't know how I was going to turn things around, but I knew I could. By the time the seminar was over there was no doubt in my mind that I was exactly where I had needed to be. I knew exactly why I needed to be there and had an inspiration for how I was going to start over."

I'm all for the power of positive thinking and do believe we subconsciously affect our future based on current circumstances. I had just not had the opportunity to meet someone who was so open and honest about sharing her own experience with such candour and honesty. The very fact that Gloria recognized that her own energy shift had contributed to the demise of her business, was not only humbling but courageous.

Gloria went on to describe that Life Alchemy involves working one-to-one with clients as a coach. Although this is not typical life-coaching. Her approach is really about showing her clients in very tangible ways that everything is energy and that we are each molding the clay of our lives, moment by moment through our thoughts and feelings.

Everything Gloria teaches is based on the latest in quantum physics, neuroscience and neuroplasticity. This means giving your brain the opportunity to establish new patterns and/or routines to achieve different results.

She not only has a strong conviction, but has achieved success and believes that what she teaches works, 100 per cent of the time! The certifications she received gave her insight into how she would be able to describe her approach with both tangible and intangible examples so that individuals would be able to better understand the theory. The best takeaway from the course was the rolodex of teaching stories she often uses with new clients.

The best examples are of gravity, radio frequency and email addresses. These are all built on a scientific formula, which we don't question. If we send an individual an email, we don't worry that it will be received by someone else! If we listen to our favourite radio station, we don't expect to hear the music from another channel! These are things that we can't explain yet we instinctively believe. This is the basis of quantum physics. It may be something we can't explain but for the most part, we don't question the science.

In practical terms, we need to understand that everything is energy and that, with the laws governing energy, we have the power and ability to take control of our lives and create whatever we'd love to create.

We can literally learn how to mold and bend reality.

Gloria often uses a quote that explains her theory:

"Reality is merely an illusion, albeit a persistent one."
– Albert Einstein

One of Gloria's clients shares her experience through this testimonial:

"Life-changing and positive!"

"My experience with Life Alchemy has truly been life-changing in a very positive and enlightening way. Gloria has taught me how to harness and create my own energy to make things happen in my life, and I have now experienced the results first-hand! Gloria uses her own real-life experience to anchor in the lessons, and this makes it more easily understood and then applied. Highly recommended Life Alchemy for both personal and business transformations!"

This is very positive, thought-provoking and a testament to the fact that this works 100 per cent of the time. It may be a leap of faith for some, but you can't argue with the results.

When Gloria begins any new business relationship she is looking for clients, who are really looking for significant shifts and changes in their lives and are committed to personal transformation. She starts off introducing clients to the basic concepts of energy.

Through the use of various tools, she demonstrates that their thoughts and feelings can move physical matter and that where our attention goes, the energy flows. A visual picture conveys that, we are all senders and receivers of electro-magnetic frequencies (like radio and TV stations) and this assists with making the connection between the concepts and reality. Quantum physics shows us that like frequencies cohere, and dislike frequencies dissipate. If we want to create new results in our lives, we have to shift our frequency so that new and different people, circumstances and events cohere to us creating new results.

When we take 100 per cent responsibility for our lives we have freedom. It's a paradox. Taking responsibility becomes freedom. When we take total responsibility we recognize we have created the lemons. In her own life, she can look back and see that she is a very powerful creator. If she could create a seemingly huge disaster, all it takes is a shift in frequency to create a huge success. A mere shift in your vibration turns lemons into lemonade.

As part of the foundational elements in a new client relationship, Gloria teaches this 3-step creative process:

Step 1: Define Your Dream
Through a series of exercises and questions, she helps people gain clarity on what it is they'd really like to create. Clients come away from this process with an awareness of exactly what they are looking for. They create a vision for their business/ work/vocation and a mission, or soul-signature, for their life's purpose and passion. These are revisited and fine tuned throughout their work together.

Step 2: Flow Energy to Your Dream
She gives clients numerous tools to focus energy on what they'd like to create, raising their vibration on a daily and consistent basis. Part of this process is teaching clients

how to set intentions and see them manifested. Much of the work together is done in Step 2, so you become a master at intentionally creating your life by design.

Step 3: The Law of GOYA (Get Off Your A**)
This is about taking action but only taking action AFTER you have defined your dream through clear intensions and flowed energy to it. When you've followed Step 1 and Step 2, Step 3 is about taking inspired action and creating from a place that is full of ELFS.

Easy   **L**ucrative   **F**un   **S**atisfying

We combine this 3-step process with her word of advice:
Choice!
Choice!!
Choice!!!

You are bound to experience results.

"In every moment of every day, you and I are creating our lives. We don't get a choice as to whether or not we create. We do! If we breathe for another 365 days, we will have created another year in the journey. The only question is, are you choosing to co-create your life consciously, by design, or are you creating by default? Either way, it's a choice."

This is one of her favourite quotes:

"The basis of life is freedom, and the result of life is expansion – but the purpose of your life is joy."
- Esther Hicks

In every moment we have the freedom to choose. And we're choosing consciously and subconsciously. We can choose joy, or sorrow and misery; love or hate; jealousy and revenge; freedom or bondage; abundance or lack; vibrant health or disease and suffering; peace and harmony or anxiety and stress; life or death.

Her motto: "Choose the life you want to live!"

This is really powerful stuff and as I listened to Gloria share her experience I couldn't but help to be affected and reflect on our own situation to decide if we are in fact living our authentic lives.

As part of the discussion, I was curious to hear how she was able to find clients that shared her theories and beliefs. After all, the concepts she shares are not for the faint of heart. In fact, some may find them hard to believe.

Gloria admitted that by far, the strongest source of new clients is from referrals. Eighty to ninety per cent of her new business directly comes from existing clients. She has a website and uses LinkedIn, Facebook and Twitter to expand her reach and provide insight into her core principles. These are effective tools that open the doors to new opportunities and potential clients.

The best source for new revenue? She practices what she preaches! She sets intentions for what she wants to create in her business by focusing energy to draw those people who are open and receptive to what she has to offer, with the capacity and willingness to pay for it.

And IT WORKS!

As a "solopreneur" she takes inspired action, which means that she does not spin her wheels on busy work and marketing that will not yield significant results. She is very aware and conscious about the type of marketing she chooses, which usually finds itself rooted in a foundation of public speaking. This gives her the opportunity to share her philosophy with a large audience, where she can connect with individuals who are interested in the one-to-one sessions. This is a great advertising opportunity that pays dividends while at the same time sharing her experience and giving people things to ponder for their own future. It is a very personal business and the connection with the client is paramount to his or her personal success. Gloria is very clear that her clients' success is based on their own goals and objectives. She guides them through Step 1, 2 and 3 providing them with the tools to achieve their own success after choosing their own journeys.

When speaking in public Gloria has the chance to provide thought leadership on the power of positive energy. Individuals participate in an exercise that demonstrates the power of their own energy within the comfort and anonymity of being in a crowd or with their peers.

This gives anyone who is interested in learning a choice!

Throughout her own career, working with the power of energy can be invigorating, but also presents its own challenge to be on your game when working with clients. To continue to nurture her own energy source she believes in the concept of life-long learning. Inspiration or motivation comes from nature and connecting with people, books, webinars, workshops, and seminars.

It was no surprise that she also has a routine and commitment to daily meditation. She has developed her own practice, making a conscious contact with source, or the divine on a daily basis. Regardless of religion, she believes that each of us has a deep knowingness within us, and that we can reach out to connect with this force at any time. Her commitment to mediation provides her with a personal source of renewable energy and strong connection with source on a daily basis.

When you combine this renewable energy exercise with the thrill and excitement she experiences when witnessing a client's personal success, it illustrates the one two formula for her own motivation.

When working with clients who experience shifts and breakthroughs, the energy exchange is reciprocal, providing both Gloria and the client with additional inspiration and motivation.

Some clients are experiencing business and financial success like never before, and share in their own enthusiasm and positive energy, which helps to fuel her energy. One client doubled her business within four months, while making the conscious choice to change and understand her own potential. Multiple clients have dramatically grown their businesses and their incomes with ease, joy, and fun. Many have attracted their perfect partners, while others have simply increased their enjoyment in life.

There really is no limit to your own success when you make the commitment to change and work with someone who can help you achieve your goals.

Gloria has found a perfect way to partner with her clients as they change their own Life Alchemy!

Gloria's Highlights:

1) Three words of advice?
   Choice, Choice, Choice

2) Breaking barriers?
   Making lemonade out of lemons by articulating to a prospective client the concept of quantum physics and how it can dramatically change their life.

3) The most satisfying moment?
   Working with clients who begin to see results and enjoyment.

Gloria MacDonald / Life Alchemy Inc.

For more than 20 years, Gloria MacDonald has worked with organizations and individuals, helping them build their dreams, accelerate their results, and create richer, more fulfilling lives. She literally teaches people how to shift their energy and create their lives consciously, by design, rather than by default.

MacDonald is a creative business woman who has built a successful brand with multiple line extensions. She hosted her own weekly TV show and radio show and has been featured in numerous national newspapers and magazines.

Gloria is an international speaker, educator, motivator, author and renowned relationship expert. She is a highly successful entrepreneur who has had the privilege of studying with some of the thought leaders in the fields of Neuroplasticity, Quantum Physics and Personal Development. She is a certified Dream Builder Coach and Life Mastery Consultant through the Life Mastery Institute.

Gloria is committed to sharing her knowledge and experiences with the world.

www.gloriamacdonald.com

Networking – Your Circle of Influence
Building Your Personal Tribe
Martha Henderson
Independent Consultant, Arbonne

Martha Henderson is a Canadian Olympic athlete. She belongs to a very distinguished group of individuals who have represented our country through sport and international competition. Her Olympic experience was in Beijing, 2008 in Women's Sailing, Keelboat (Yngling Class). Her team finished 13th overall.

The Olympics take centre stage, and the world for a time unites through the spirit and energy of athleticism. As a nation, we are proud of the athletes who represent our country and demonstrate a commitment to become best in class. Teamwork is the foundation when going for the gold and building a circle of influence is part of the strategy for success.

Martha's journey was life-changing, character-building and entrepreneurial. She was a full-time athlete for six years before going back into the world of business after the Olympic Games.

When she first began sailing it was not in pursuit of an Olympic dream but rather to explore a passion for the sport. "I was never the best sailor – actually I spent the first few years of sailing camp lying in the bottom of the boat, singing songs and having fun. Many years later, I found an evaluation my instructor wrote about me that said I was a pushy airhead and would not go anywhere in sailing. I love that! Sailing is my passion and my love for the sport is why I excelled."

On the national team, Martha had to coordinate her own planning, shipping, fundraising, travel arrangements and equipment development, as well as hiring coaches and trainers. It was through this experience that she began to hone her entrepreneurial skills. The sport is not structured by the federation to assist with these functions, so the athletes have both the flexibility and opportunity to plan for their events, either as an individual or team.

When describing her Olympic experience, Martha often refers to a personal quality: perseverance. "If perseverance is part of your DNA, then opportunities will present themselves to give you what you need at just the right time." Having a team in alignment with the same goals and dreams is when the magic happens. It takes time to develop that spirit. While there may be setbacks along the way, if you believe in your dream and where you're going, the team will come together and the magic will follow.

It was through this experience that Martha began to appreciate the efforts of her team and understood that working together so much more can be accomplished than that of one individual. Participating as a member of a team, you not only learn to work towards a common goal, but develop qualities that are beneficial in the future. Skills such as listening, discipline, problem-solving and handling disappointment all lead to the positive energy and excitement you feel whether you win or lose.

What Martha did not realize until going back into the corporate world was how entrepreneurial she had become. At the time, the natural progression was to get a job to begin to pay for the debt she had acquired after almost six years of full-time sailing. After four years behind a desk, Martha realized that she had become a spectator in her own life and that she had to make a change. At the time, there was no master plan, but she was looking for a challenging team environment where she'd use the skills and experience she'd developed as an athlete in a business environment. She recalled something during her first interview when training for the Olympics. One of her training partners stated: "The important thing is the journey not the outcome. If you embrace the journey, then the outcome will definitely be sweet."

Martha agrees with the sentiment as she comes from an entrepreneurial family – in fact, two generations of entrepreneurs. "I guess we have never been very good at waiting for others to give us permission to get something done." If you appreciate the road that takes you through success, then you will enjoy the journey along the way.

It was with this attitude that after almost two years as a customer with Arbonne that she found her entrepreneurial venture. After attending a number of Arbonne events, Martha was introduced to people who were happy, shared goals and dreams, while doing something positive for themselves and their families. She then decided to join Arbonne, a U.S.-based network-marketing leader that manufactures and distributes Swiss-formulated skin care, cosmetics and weight-loss products.

"I was in place where my salary was frozen with no opportunity for advancement. At the time, I was thinking about getting a part-time job to have some additional income. What I realized was that I could have my own company on my own time setting goals and receiving compensation for my effort. I could also build a team and teach people how to have their own businesses. The low start-up cost and ability to work on my own schedule was just the right thing for me."

The business philosophy of this multi-level marketing company provides the products and/or services to connect to a niche market, with marketing support to build a strong client base within a solid framework for success. You can adapt a retail model for sales in pursuit of income. Founder Petter Morck's vision for the company demonstrates its commitment to success: "Arbonne is a place where ordinary people do extraordinary things, not only to enhance their own lives, but also the lives of many others." Those who participate in the business network share the same personal and professional mission, which gives everyone the chance to be successful. The power of this common goal demonstrates the entrepreneurial spirit.

If you draw a parallel in sailing, Martha and her teammates were very different individuals. There was an 18-year age difference between the youngest and the oldest member of the team. What brought them together was a shared vision and the ability to celebrate their own skills which were complementary to each other and the team. These combined skills contributed to the team's success.

This similar concept applies to Arbonne – where they support, encourage and promote success through celebrating the individual, while enhancing the efforts of each individual on the team.

Ideally, you build your team with like-minded individuals. Everyone can work at his or her own pace, adjust their own schedule and contribute by sharing individual experiences.

One of Martha's philosophies is to present opportunities to other individuals, who may be interested in creating their own success journey. This creates win-win relationships and long-term strategic partnerships.

Personal Vision/Mission Statement:
"To create opportunities for people to do spectacular things, so that they can participate in life and not be a spectator."

Martha believes each individual can "grasp the power of their own journey" and enhance their lives in many different ways through the support of the company. Martha strives to create the magic she experienced when sailing with her Arbonne team. She has weekly conference calls sharing challenges and success stories, which often are a reminder that there is no glass ceiling within the company. You can become as successful as you wish, "It's your choice." Martha also shares a "tip of the week" through a recorded message, available to everyone on the extended team.

The leadership skills that Martha learned throughout her Olympic experience have been very beneficial, and she draws these parallels between athletics and business:

1) Listening skills have increased her ability to provide solutions
2) Adapting to course conditions creates the mindset for strategic planning and welcoming change
3) Testing different techniques while training for the Olympics created a strong work ethic and the tenacity to keep moving forward
4) Being part of the magic has enhanced her ability to coach others
5) Winning and losing has provided a foundation to enjoy the journey

When Martha first began her entrepreneurial experience she connected with many different people in order to find individuals who would become part of her team. Her mandate is to create win-win relationships. As an example, when going on a business trip or travelling on a holiday, instead of putting on her headphones and listening to music she will often start a conversation with the people sitting next to her. It is amazing to hear their personal stories and sometimes it's as simple as connecting them with someone she knows who may be able to assist with their own personal journey. She believes in being a participant rather than a spectator!

If you have ever heard the quote by Jim Rohn, "You are the average of the five people you spend the most time with," then, by extension, your circle of influence will have a tremendous impact on your goals and objectives.

Martha has the support of many individuals within the Arbonne network to assist with her business success, but she contributes her positive energy to her own circle of influence:

1. **Personal Partner:** – Her boyfriend and best friend. Jeff is also self employed and supports her 100 per cent in both her sailing and business. He reminds her when she's impatient: "Having your own business is not a sprint, but rather a marathon."

2. **Business Coach**: – The work on mindset and energy has not only dramatically improved her business, but also her overall happiness and well-being.

3. **Role Model:** – **Team leader at Arbonne**. Amy is one of the most successful people in the company and is the most open, welcoming and generous person. As a role model, she is accessible as part of the Arbonne family and provides inspiration on how to run a truly successful business – with humour, grace and intelligence!

4 & 5. **Family Support: Mom and Dad** – Martha sailed with her father for 10 years, competing both locally and internationally. He taught her the ropes, laying a solid foundation in perseverance and leadership. Her mother is both encouraging and supportive, always there from the beginning of her career right through to the Olympics. She did everything from towing her team out to the race course, driving to Florida – three boats in tow and the car packed to

the hilt – to standing on the dock every day as they sailed out to the races at the Olympic Games, waving a Canadian Flag. "It still makes me teary," she recalls. The philosophy is true; Martha has been influenced by the people with whom she shares her life and they have contributed to her current spirit and positive energy.

If you were to ask Martha for three words of advice she would say: "Embrace the journey."

"If you are just working for the pay cheque, promotion or for the Gold Medal then you will be let down. The journey is where you receive the most growth and development. The friends and experiences you have along the way are what make life rich!"

The team at Arbonne provide the platform for success by giving you the tools for a solid foundation. One of the many benefits of this model is flexibility. Flexibility, not only in time, but in a cost-effective opportunity for growth. The technology provided by an international company makes it so easy to have a global business with little or low cost. Online platforms that provide face-to-face access with people across Canada and the globe allow for the possibility of having a 24-hour, 365-days-a-year business without having to leave the comfort of your own home (unless of course you want to.) It's simply amazing!

The freedom that aligns itself with flexibility is one of the factors that attracted Martha to the business model. Working in an office became too structured and restrictive after her Olympic experience. The freedom she experienced while training for eight years gave her the flexibility to enjoy the journey. What she realized when meeting other members of the Arbonne team was that the opportunities available are limited only by your own strategic goals. There is no glass ceiling!

Combine the entrepreneurial spirit with the collaboration of the team and Martha feels you are guaranteed success. Hard work is part of the equation and a familiar part of her DNA as an athlete. Taking these skills and applying them to a tested business model gives you the chance to fill in the blanks with a strong team to enjoy the rewards. You can also choose your own retail model, based on your specific market area and target market. It is not a cookie cutter approach, and Martha has chosen a one-to-one presentation style that allows her to not only get to know her customers, but customize their experience, resulting in prequalified referrals.

Martha remembers the day she decided to pursue her own business:

"My boyfriend asked me to introduce a friend of his to my Arbonne friends since she was looking for additional income. I asked him how he knew about Arbonne(!)? He told me that I talked about it all the time! I was not aware that I talked about it that much, but if this was the case and he had someone who was interested in being involved, then I was going to get involved and see where it took me.

I called my friend, with whom I had hosted an event, we had lunch, I jumped in and never looked back!"

As part of the journey Martha, talks about the magic that follows when a team is working together towards the same goal. In her experience, when everyone on the team shares the same vision with a clear plan it creates that magic. It is Martha's personal brand of magic that creates and encourages a commitment to her business team, and it becomes both rewarding and satisfying.

As you find business builders who are as interested in a shared goal as part of your team you are able to enjoy the journey that leads to mutual success.

Who doesn't want to become - not only part of a successful team but realize her own goals and objectives? Arbonne provides support, flexibility and structure for a successful business, and on Martha's team they strive for the magic.

From Olympic athlete to entrepreneur, seizing opportunity and taking action is what has given Martha the formula to enjoy life and appreciate her journey.

Taking the time to introduce other would-be entrepreneurs to this business model ensures that everyone has the opportunity to enjoy their success, both individually and as part of the team.

What other business platform offers this model for success?

Martha will admit "it's not for everyone," but in her experience, whether going for the gold, or simply enjoying the journey, Martha and her team appreciate the magic.

Martha's Highlights:

1) Three words of advice?
   "Embrace the journey."

2) Breaking barriers?
   "After 4 years of being chained to a desk, I realized that I had become a spectator in my own life and needed to make a change." Working as part of the Arbonne team provides limitless potential.

3) The most satisfying moment?
   "Realizing I could have my own company on my own time, setting goals and being compensated for my effort."

Martha Henderson / Arbonne

Martha Henderson has had a varied and interesting background. She translated a degree in English into a career in sports and promotional marketing working for International Management Group as well as other large sporting events and companies along with a stint in advertising and in the cultural world.

In 2000, changes to the Olympic Sailing program opened the opportunity for Martha to pursue her life long passion of sailing in the Olympics. She focused on this goal and qualified to represent Canada at the 2008 Olympic Games in Beijing when she was 40 years old.

After the Olympics, Martha went back into the corporate world but knew that there was more that she could do with all of the skills.

When the opportunity arose to start her own Network Marketing business, Martha was unsure but intrigued. Once she realized this was the opportunity that she had been looking for, she grabbed it and ran with it.

www.marthahenderson.arbonne.ca

Expanding Your Territory
The Confidence Game
Your Roadmap to Expansion
Virginia Burt – Virginia Burt Designs Inc.

Virginia Burt, of Virginia Burt Designs Inc. is an award-winning landscape architect. Her firm has been involved in a wide range of projects, including designing therapeutic gardens for hospitals and institutions, estate master plans, and native landscape restoration in both Canada and the United States.

She is one of only six women recognized by her peers through the awarding of a fellowship from both the Canadian and American Societies of Landscape Architects. Fellowship is conferred upon individuals in recognition of exceptional accomplishments over a sustained period of time.

Virginia's philosophy is grounded in the idea that gardens can engage the mind, body, spirit and emotions within a deep experience of the natural environment. She believes that landscapes and gardens, both large and small, whether urban or rural, remote or in the downtown core, play a huge role in human health. She is passionate about creating spaces where people, art and nature intersect. Throughout the design process she encourages collaboration with her team, clients, architects and other allied professionals.

Virginia melds the spirit of each site found through a thoughtful analysis of existing conditions with the needs and desires of the client, to create beautiful and meaningful landscapes.

If you visit her website, you'll notice her company, Virginia Burt Designs Inc., has received many awards and recognition from peers.

When you speak with Virginia she is very candid that her road to success has been paved with many special moments where individuals referred her to projects that have lead to a unique niche market of "healing gardens."

When I first met Virginia, I noticed she had an energetic spirit and zest for life, couched in a humble and grateful personal philosophy. She has a special quality of making YOU feel important when engaging her in conversation. I was fascinated to hear why she had chosen this particular profession and when I asked, she immediately shared her personal story about the time she decided she wanted to be a landscape architect.

"I chose this profession because it was a calling. I have my brother to thank for this; he brought home a friend in the landscape architecture program at the University of Guelph for a family Thanksgiving. I was completely fascinated that there was a program that would combine my love of the outdoors, art and interest in a firm grounding for how things are made. I immediately arranged a tour of the school and was hooked. That was in Grade 11 and I haven't looked back. As part of the experience, the entrepreneurial spirit was engendered by my family – I was encouraged and supported to do those things that made me happy. This was the result of a wonderful family environment. Growing up on an apple farm until age 10 taught me the value of hard work and a great appreciation of watching things grow. At every turn, my mother encouraged me as a young female professional. My father would quietly sit me down and ask specific questions that helped me to formulate the next steps in my own plan."

This support and vision was part of a foundation that built a successful business, which combines natural talent with the conviction to do what she loves, and translate this energy into a long term career.

As entrepreneurs, we build on our knowledge and education as a solid foundation, and soon realize we have to sell our product and service as an important part of our success. In fact, you don't really have a business until you have someone who is able to sell what you offer to a client interested in paying your price or fee. A background in sales will support and sustain a long-term commitment to a strategic business plan that is critical to both personal and financial success.

Sales is often one area of business that is taken for granted and it will change, evolve and morph throughout time and your career. For some, it can be challenging. For others, it is as natural as the decision to start your own company. If you believe in your success, it is ultimately something you need to embrace.

To build her comprehension of the role of sales, Virginia, began to take courses and facilitation training. Her natural enthusiasm and approach had taken her a long way however it was time for the next level. A documented sales process and her natural approach when asking for both sales and referrals have become the building blocks throughout her career. She has a commitment to life-long learning and always being open to something new.

Her first project in the U.S. demonstrates the many opportunities that have been presented throughout the years. Early in her own business, Virginia attended a course on facilitation techniques. She attended feeling that it would assist with her ability to make formal presentations as part of the design/sales process. There was a unique cross-section of people in attendance and when it was her turn to present, one woman was intrigued with her content and delivery. The woman happened to be on the board of a spiritual retreat in the United States, looking for a landscape master plan. It just so happened, she was having a board meeting that evening and, as they were in the process of selecting a landscape architect, she put Virginia's name forward for the project. Shortly thereafter, Virginia went on a driving trip to visit the site and meet with the selection committee. At the end of her trip they invited her to submit a proposal for the retreat, and to her delight, her firm received the commission for the project. To her further amazement, Virginia Burt Designs later won a national award for the planning work on the project from The American Society of Landscape Architects in 1999.

First time lucky or serendipity?

Virginia will be the first to admit that her career has been a series of these special moments, and she accredits this success to being open to opportunities wherever and whenever they may present themselves, being able to recognize the prospect and take action. She believes in being passionate about your work and has a strong conviction that when you give your word, you deliver and commit to following through on your promise. The success with this first U.S. project led to other award-winning opportunities in healing gardens that over the past 20 years has culminated in creating a niche market and opening an office in Ohio, United States.

Her firm is now considered international.

By any standards Virginia's career is indeed successful. However, the road to entrepreneurship and owning her own business was not as smooth as you may think, and there is no one who tells the story better than Virginia about her own "ah ha" moment.

"For 11 years after graduation, I had worked for two large professional firms. At the same time I had pursued various volunteer, and personal development paths. When the second firm invited me to become a partner, looking around the table, I realized that although the people were friends, I wouldn't choose them as business partners. And with that, I started a landscape architecture department within a different planning firm, thinking it would be more in alignment with my beliefs of creating a greener world. This frankly did not work.

Divergent beliefs, and a developer client focus, added up to a great level of discomfort. On the evening that I packed my boxes into my car leaving that job, I was willing to wait on tables before I would practice landscape architecture in the same way. It so happened, I was volunteering for a facilitation process that evening. It was called *World Council*. They had a motto of "accessing greatness within to act with greatness outside of yourself." At the break, a woman approached me to say thank you for volunteering. Her question: "What is it that you do in your real job?" To this day, I am astonished at my impromptu response: "I am a landscape architect and I design spirit and healing gardens." There was a moment of silence when the woman turned and said "wow tell me more about that..." I was in shock and an epiphany had occurred when making that statement from the heart. This happened on June 12, 1996. The following evening I shared this story at a dinner table with friends. The gentleman sitting across from me turned and said "I would like a garden like that." He became my first client and I started Virginia Burt Designs on June 13, 1996."

Serendipity?

"Healing gardens" is a term Virginia feels can be applied to any garden, depending on the wishes of the client. To her, every space she creates can be or become a place of healing, where people enjoy the moment and experience the landscape using all of their five senses – taste, see, hear, touch, and smell.

When a garden is specifically designed as a healing garden for a person with a particular disease or condition, the spatial relationships, plant materials, accessibility, textures and scents (to a name a few) all coexist to create a place where the patient, loved ones and staff can find a sense of respite and be drawn into the present moment.

Studies and research clearly show that even a view of nature reduces both heart rate and blood pressure. Many of these patients, family members and staff who have the opportunity to experience outdoor spaces will experience reduced stress.

It is an opportunity for people to find a place of comfort in what is a highly stressful moment.

Virginia, appreciates this dilemma and therefore takes a holistic approach when beginning the design process for a place of healing. She often conducts a site visit where she can not only see, but feel the space and assess the current environment and location using her own five senses.

The designated space can, at times, be challenging as it is not always the primary focus for the business or location. Some are on rooftops, courtyards or tight, cozy nooks, where creating something beautiful offers individuals a unique experience to view and appreciate their surroundings. Think of a hospital where patients, family, friends and staff can take a few moments to sit in a beautiful, calm, and inviting space. It offers a place to decompress while in a challenging atmosphere, and offers a different dimension or reason for their visit.

Virginia is often asked: "Is there a particular plant or plant material traditionally found in a healing garden?" She smiles and explains that when she begins the design process, she visualizes the space and through thoughtful conversation with the client, begins the creative process by adding a visual perspective to the design. You say words and she interprets those words into pictures! The design follows suit.

Her holistic approach builds on the emotional realm and Virginia uses the *Seven Landscape Archetypes* (Julie Moir Messervy, 1996) as part of her creative process. These elements spatially affect garden visitors at any level (physical, mental, emotional or spiritual) and maximize the healing potential.

The 7 Landscape Archetypes

There are seven distinct landscape archetypes that we experience in the way spaces feel. These archetypes were originally developed by Julie Moir Messervy. Landscapes that incorporate all, or many, of the seven archetypes give people of all ages a choice of any spatial environment that they want to experience.

1) The Sea – Immersion

2) The Cave – Nestling

3) The Harbour – Embracing

4) The Promontory – Extension

5) The Island – Separateness

6) The Mountain –Transformation

7) The Sky –Transcendence

These archetypes guide the conversation so that Virginia is able to see the design that her clients describe through their thoughts and words.

Combining these tools creates a place for vision, inspiration and motivation.

Coincidence or serendipity?

It is no secret when you begin a business that part of your success is your ability to sell your products or services. After all, as an entrepreneur YOU are synonymous with the business.

The sales process can become personal because the prices you charge are a direct reflection of you and your professional ability. Many struggle with the concept of price and developing a pricing structure, which aligns with having a sense of your value or worth in the market.

These foundational elements ground your business through a connection with your client, and the prices you charge for goods and/or services begin the legacy for your professional reputation.

In Virginia's business she provides both – services via creative ideas or "blue-prints" for a project, and goods through softscape – or plant materials and hardscape with the building of retaining walls, water features, paved terraces, planting containers etc.

Virginia uses a line that couched in humour sets the stage when discussing professional fees. "No one has ever said that I am the least expensive!"

Kudos to her in having a true sense of her firm's worth in the market and being able to secure business based on her reputation, years of experience and creative talent.

After all, she will readily admit if you are considered too expensive or overpriced, the proposals you submit will not translate into successful projects.

So how did she arrive at a pricing structure that would allow her to secure business on both sides of the border without the fear of being too expensive?

"First of all, fear doesn't come into it. I am firm in my conviction that we provide excellent services so our rates reflect that conviction. When validating my own theory I began to speak with other business professionals to understand their philosophy on fees or price. A colleague once said to me she planned to charge $100 per hour. Asking why the rate would be so low, she responded that was what the market would bear. I further inquired and wondered if her services were on par with other local colleagues; interestingly enough her response was no! – she provides much better service! At that moment, I think she realized she could and should increase her hourly fee. When digging deeper into other professional services, and upon researching the legal profession, a friend of the same age and experience charged $695 per hour. Interesting. I then looked at my car repair bill, my mechanic charged $120 per hour and a plumber with 30 years of experience charged $150 per hour. It soon became clear that my experience, conviction and services priced appropriately would attract the right kinds of clients."

A sound theory based on her own informal research.

Virginia's conviction and philosophy about her business has also been influenced by a dear friend and mentor, Cornelia Hahn Oberlander. When she speaks of Cornelia, it is with a tremendous amount of admiration and respect. In fact, she shared with me that Cornelia graduated as one of the first female landscape architects at Harvard University in the United States. At the age of 94, she is still producing, lecturing and traveling to do her work. Cornelia provides inspiration and helps Virginia to clarify her vision of what's next or even what not to do.

Cornelia's motto of success is summarized by the five Ps: Politeness, Professionalism, Patience, Passion, and Persistence. She is truly an inspiration and role model for young people looking to become designers. Cornelia's years of experience add perspective when brainstorming about new ideas and concepts. This too has an influence when developing strategic direction or plans for expansion.

Through this friendship, Virginia has adopted Cornelia's credo, summarized into the acronym VIM: Vision, Imagination, Motivation. These guiding principles provide the building blocks of Virginia's personal goal to create a greener world founded in a belief that people can thrive socially, spiritually, physically, mentally and emotionally. It ties her corporate philosophy to her personal beliefs.

Vision
Having the ability to visualize the finished projects as well as success will provide a solid foundation. A clear intention for the future will create a powerful environment and Virginia has learned that "this stuff works."

At an event celebrating New Year's, close to midnight, Virginia had each guest reflect upon the past year. Then they were invited to write an intention on a small piece of paper for the coming year and send it out into the universe by burning it in the fire.

Of course, Virginia wrote her intention and happily threw it on the fire without a backwards glance. At 9 a.m. the following morning she received an email out of the blue that asked if she would be interested in a project – the exact type of client, project and place that she had articulated on her small piece of paper!

Serendipity or conviction?

Imagination
As with any creative business Virginia finds inspiration in various aspects of everyday life that fuels her imagination, while being grounded and connected to the earth. Reading, traveling and participating in outside activities like sailing, skiing and hiking all contribute to her creativity.

Her imagination leads to the design ideas that she presents to clients as they begin a new project. When she meets with a client or family, the dialogue that eventually follows taps into their imagination, and through conversation, these ideas ultimately lead to the finished design.

She "sees" the words her client describes. Collaboration and synergy can and will push the creative envelope, allowing her to explore her imagination that ultimately leads to her best work.

Motivation
Throughout her career Virginia had made a commitment to ongoing personal development and facilitation training. As a visual learner, this includes creating vision boards with clarity of intention.

Each day presents a new challenge and being clear on your intensions will help to motivate you for the next level of success.

Virginia is famous for her little sayings that simply define certain elements of entrepreneurship. I have heard her say, "I'm dealing with the alligators in the swamp today." That creates a clear visual that requires no further conversation;

but is always said with a little chuckle and you just know that finding the solution will motivate her towards another day.

The challenges and solutions contribute to her own roadmap of success, which fuels both her positive energy and commitment to believe that tomorrow will be a better, brighter day.

In fact, maybe the alligators will swim somewhere else tomorrow!

Serendipity, through a sense of humour?

Speaking of alligators...

As with any business, there's always an element that's particularly challenging.

As part of her ongoing training and personal development, Virginia knew that understanding financial documents was a huge hurdle and she had to commit to dealing with when she met with her accountant or bookkeeper.

It was all fine, and well to have a fee structure and sales process under control but she needed to be able to acutely analyze the numbers, which appeared on her balance sheet and/or profit and loss statement.

She realized that spreadsheets were a meaningless sea of numbers. The quarterly financial review was not something she looked forward to and it was becoming an obstacle in her enjoyment of being self-employed.

After a great deal of trial and error it suddenly occurred to her, as a visual learner, why not ask for the numbers to be shown as a coloured graph? This would give her the opportunity to see her progress at a glance and identify areas that needed further discussion or review.

Of course, her team was more than happy to provide the visual perspective. Once complete, she was able to quickly grasp the concept, even if some of the individual numbers needed further explanation.

As an added bonus, her life partner is a financial wizard who provided ongoing guidance to assist with clearly connecting the dots between the numbers and the graphs.

As far as Virginia is concerned, challenges are part of being a business owner and in order to overcome a challenge, you need to be persistent, find a trusted advisor or colleague to help and just keep learning.

The frustration she was experiencing was admitting to a fear of being wrong, combined with an inability to decipher the complex numbers that comprised her financial statements.

The solution in this case wasn't taking another business course or reading another book that would eventually collect dust because it wasn't interesting; instead, it became a challenge or task to be resolved rather than charged with emotional angst.

The coloured graph provided her with the visual she needed to further discuss the numbers associated with each section of the financials.

This gave her the confidence to ask the right questions and receive the answers required to make sound, strategic decisions for her continued business plan.

As an added bonus, finding her equilibrium in the sales department lead to a better understanding of the financials.

It may not be the most enjoyable part of her business, but she recognized that it was a necessary evil or "alligator in the swamp." Now it has simply become part of any strategic discussion and annual planning session.

Here are a few sales tips that Virginia has found relevant when operating a business with two separate offices in two different countries:

1) Organization
Finding tools that will enhance your ability to be organized will lead to greater efficiency.

2) Dynamic Calendar
Creating a routine that allows for change will provide the flexibility required to meet deadlines and project demands. This is a fluid process and in sync with the sales and projects associated with each office.

3) Synergy
This is a conduit to finding the connection between the people and place that will ensure the right fit. Sometimes you may need to walk away from a sale because it does not meet your corporate or personal philosophy regardless of the fee.

4) Thought Leadership/Mentorship
Being able to brainstorm your ideas with a trusted advisor has lead to increased confidence and a strong conviction to be comfortable with each business decision that's in the best interest of her team and the firm.

5) Strategic Planning
Without a roadmap you will be unable to realize your goals and objectives. Having a master plan that includes sales volume and the type of work, interests both you and your firm.

If there is one takeaway from Virginia and her sales experience it is a strong conviction to be true to your core values.

If your gut instinct tells you to walk away, then, with confidence, she will bow out of a project.

Combine this intuitiveness with her ongoing commitment to life-long learning and you have a foundation to hone your personal skills, which reflects back to her adopted acronym VIM.

Vision, Imagination and Motivation becomes part of the annual strategic plan that includes not only the sales discussion, but sow the seed that needs to be planted for another successful year.

Virginia's Highlights:

1) Three words of advice?
VIM = Vision, Imagination, Motivation.

2) Breaking Barriers?
Understanding financial documents.

3) The most satisfying moment?
Her ah ha moment and realizing there was a better way of doing business while achieving her personal and professional goals.

Virginia Burt / Virginia Burt Designs Inc.

Virginia Burt, FCSLA, FASLA creates landscapes and gardens of meaning for residential clients, healthcare facilities and unique special projects. Her love of the land has been a lifetime journey. Having grown up on an apple farm, she developed a passion for being outside and understanding the rhythms of nature. Virginia graduated with honours in landscape architecture from University of Guelph in 1985 and worked in Aspen, CO and Toronto, ON offices before starting her Virginia Burt Designs firm in 1996.

For over 30 years Virginia's international award-winning work has been recognized in the design of healing gardens, labyrinths and sacred spaces. In 2015, Virginia was elevated to Fellow in both the Canadian Society of Landscape Architects (CSLA) and the American Society of Landscape Architects (ASLA). Recent awards include the National CSLA Award of Merit in 2015 and a 2014 Palladio Award in USA and she has been published and has presented over 200 conferences across North America.

Virginia's design work reflects her roots, creating gardens and landscapes that reveal their natural context and reflect those who use them. Clients appreciate and value her deep respect for place and for the human dimensions of each project. Virginia gets things built – beautifully.

www.vburtdesigns.com

Life Experience

When I began to write this book, I took a leap of faith that I would be able to connect with 10 entrepreneurial women who would share their story and provide insight into not only their business, but their own life experiences.

A few of the participants were ladies I had met throughout the years and were interested in the project, others connected through introductions that have led to friendships that I will cherish in the years to come.

The criteria was mentorship, innovation, entrepreneurship and philanthropy.

We meet periodically, so that we could begin our own network of support, sharing stories and ideas that would ultimately lead to increasing business experience and expanding our personal sphere of influence.

We have been able to support each other along the way, and because of our diverse business experiences have found that when we meet we each take away a little nugget of information.

As part of the support network, we refer potential customers and connect other women in business, who may be able to assist with a problem, provide a new perspective or share their own recipe for success.

At our first dinner meeting the energy was electric and we all walked away with a sense of ownership for this project and its continued success.

I'd like to share a few things that I have learned by meeting and interviewing these amazing ladies. Funnily enough, they all have similar experiences and, due to their commitment of honesty and integrity, share the same personal and professional values.

We all share in the following:

1) Breaking Barriers
2) Building Relationships
3) Face Challenges
4) Experience Failure
5) Believe in Innovation
6) Demonstrate Integrity
7) Continue with Life Long Learning
8) Provide Mentorship
9) Give back through Philanthropy
10) Share a Vision

Breaking Barriers

Every single woman has had to overcome obstacles to her success. Whether personal or professional, everyone has taken a "sober second thought" to break through the glass ceiling that was presented at one stage or another in her career. Each experienced an "ah ha" moment that provided inspiration to begin a journey with many personal and professional rewards.

Build Relationships

A successful career is the culmination of many strategic partnerships that change and evolve through time and circumstances.

In order to succeed, each and every woman has understood the power of working together to assist each other in reaching the pinnacle of her career. All are open, welcoming and supportive of each other's success and look for building those special relationships that encourage each other to work towards their own unique goals and objectives.

Challenges

With true conviction the word would be "opportunity." Every challenge these women faced has lead to a course correction that has improved their business and made it stronger, more efficient and profitable. Taking the challenges presented and turning them into opportunities is a skill that every entrepreneur learns through time.

Failure

As a society we do not celebrate our failures but each of these women has experienced a set back or failure at one time or another throughout the course of her career and turned that experience into a lesson learned. This has made them stronger and smarter. Each failure adds to the bricks and mortar of their company and helps build a stronger foundation for future success.

Innovation

The corporate philosophy of each company is built on an innovative idea with a twist. These ideas set them apart from their competition and account for their strong business model. It is a continuous process, and the art of invention or reinvention is something shared by all in order to be current and relevant to their customers.

Integrity

The personal integrity of each and every entrepreneur is rock solid with a strong conviction of honesty for good measure. There is no grey area.

It's black and white for these gals. When they consider the options and make sound business decisions, it is always to err on the side of what's right with a long-term view of the future.

Life Long Learning

The list of certificates and courses resulting in awards of merit is impressive and noteworthy. To remain current and expand revenue streams every single person attends conferences, seminars and/or workshops to expand her knowledge or learn new techniques and apply business theories. Knowledge is power, and there is no limit to the opportunities presented with sound business decisions.

Mentorship

The opportunity to share information and business ideas with new entrepreneurs fuels future success. Individually or collectively everyone is interested in assisting each other to grow and prosper.

As the saying goes: "If you want something done ask a busy person." She will get the job done on time and within budget.

Everyone in this group is BUSY... Yet they will take a moment to stop, help and advise anyone who reaches out, needing a little extra assistance.

We all believe in karma and the power that returns when you take the time to help someone who has taken the time to ask for information.

Philanthropy

Supporting the community is a big part of each woman's corporate philosophy. Donations of both time and/or money to a worthy cause are part of a solid corporate strategy and "give back" to each community. Each woman has been active in various charities. As part of this effort, we will be donating the royalties I receive as the author to a charity that supports entrepreneurship.

Vision

Each and every woman had a dream and conviction to succeed. The premise is always to improve a product or service, which will enhance or benefit another, and success has followed each individual with a crystal clear vision.

We are all at different stages of our careers, some are at the beginning of their journey's and others are what you might say "seasoned," but we all come from a position of strength, courage and conviction for the future.

No one is ready to retire because we truly enjoy what we do, and although some may choose to shorten their work week, it will often be because they are sitting on a board, working with a charity or attending anther special event that will fuel their energy for another few years.

Life experience takes time and, as the years roll by, so does the level of expertise.

We all started with an idea and watched it grow and change through time into something that is personally gratifying and financially successful.

Enjoy your journey, live in the moment and share your success with friends and family!

Opportunities

In the spirit of mentorship and business innovation, Trish Tonaj has written a book sharing the stories of 10 Entrepreneurial Women. This information share will give you insight into everything from the "ah ha moments to the barriers broken" in order to pursue dreams and develop strategic plans for success.

What was the motivation for the book? Trish attended a Executive Education Certificate Program at Harvard Law School, Cambridge, Massachusetts in June of 2015 with 47 other professionals from around the world. It was unanimous, the concept of mentorship has been lost in today's fast paced, fragmented business world but the spirit of entrepreneurship is alive and well! We need to share our experiences and expertise.

The foundation for Breaking Barriers is based on mentorship, innovation philanthropy and entrepreneurship.

"We have some very dynamic ladies who share their expertise, providing insight into the reasons why they've decided to explore the risk and reward of entrepreneurship."

As part of our ongoing commitment to the spirit of innovation, the royalties from this book will be donated to women's charities that support the entrepreneurial spirit.

Trish would be happy to meet with you and your team to share the concepts, strategies and stories that create an environment of enthusiasm and innovation. Whether you own your own business, work for a large company or are interested in starting your own business venture the information share will be informative and inspirational.

Give us a call; we'd love to meet with you and your team! www.phaze2wellnes.com   Follow us on LinkedIN, Facebook and Twitter: @phaze2wellness

About the Author

Trish Tonaj "runs at Mach 2 with her hair on fire" and is clearly defined by her work. As a second act career, she has combined her entrepreneurial experience and business acumen to become a Certified Personal Trainer, Nutrition/Wellness Specialist and Certified Yoga Specialist.

As an advocate for helping individuals achieve a healthy and active lifestyle, she is an Entrepreneurial Mentor and Health and Wellness Coach. Trish has published the book *A Diary of Change 12 Personal Tools* where she shares her formula to assist individuals achieve work/life balance.

Breaking Barriers, 10 Female Entrepreneurs Share Their Stories is her second endeavour and it offers an insightful journey into mentorship, innovation and philanthropy. She has a commitment to life-long learning, is a painter, loves to travel and will readily admit that life is a "work in progress."

"Love, laugher and adventure" is her personal mantra and focus for maintaining work/life balance.

www.phaze2wellness.com

Breaking Barriers / Trish Tonaj

Manor House
www.manor-house.ca

Breaking Barriers / Trish Tonaj

Manor House
www.manor-house.ca

Breaking Barriers / Trish Tonaj

Manor House
www.manor-house.ca

Breaking Barriers / Trish Tonaj

Manor House
www.manor-house.ca

Manor House
www.manor-house.ca